RE-

Cultural Inquiry

EDITED BY CHRISTOPH F. E. HOLZHEY
AND MANUELE GRAGNOLATI

The series 'Cultural Inquiry' is dedicated to exploring how diverse cultures can be brought into fruitful rather than pernicious confrontation. Taking culture in a deliberately broad sense that also includes different discourses and disciplines, it aims to open up spaces of inquiry, experimentation, and intervention. Its emphasis lies in critical reflection and in identifying and highlighting contemporary issues and concerns, even in publications with a historical orientation. Following a decidedly cross-disciplinary approach, it seeks to enact and provoke transfers among the humanities, the natural and social sciences, and the arts. The series includes a plurality of methodologies and approaches, binding them through the tension of mutual confrontation and negotiation rather than through homogenization or exclusion.

Christoph F. E. Holzhey is the Founding Director of the ICI Berlin Institute for Cultural Inquiry. Manuele Gragnolati is Professor of Italian Literature at the Sorbonne Université in Paris and Associate Director of the ICI Berlin.

RE-
An Errant Glossary

EDITED BY CHRISTOPH F. E. HOLZHEY
AND ARND WEDEMEYER

ISBN (Print): 978-3-96558-000-8
ISBN (PDF): 978-3-96558-001-5
ISBN (EPUB): 978-3-96558-002-2
DOI: 10.25620/ci-15

Bibliographical Information of the German National Library
The German National Library lists this publication in the Deutsche Nationalbibliografie (German National Bibliography); detailed bibliographic information is available online at http://dnb.d-nb.de.

Cover design: Studio Bens with a photograph by Claudia Peppel

The paperback edition is printed by Lightning Source, Milton Keynes, UK, with the actual print location being indicated on the final page.
The digital edition can be downloaded freely at:
https://www.ici-berlin.org/oa/ci-15/.

ICI Berlin
Christinenstr. 18/19
D-10119 Berlin
info@ici-berlin.org
www.ici-berlin.org

Contents

Preface

In the realm of 'theory' — the discourse traversing academic departments and negotiating their interdisciplinary commerce —, much of the heavy lifting is done by prefix. The claim holds true, or so it may seem, for modern cultural formations in general: At some point in the nineteenth century, the Catholic church developed its habit of seeing in inconvenient aspects of modernization mere returns of ancient heresies, denouncing, for example, secular life as 'neo-pelagianism'. The prefix 'neo-' migrated beyond apologetics and drove much of the industrially enhanced historicist differentiation of 'styles' in architecture and visual culture ('neogothic' being the most prominent), spreading through many cultural realms well into philosophy ('neokantianism', 'neohegelianism', etc.).[1] The twentieth century added the no less emblematic prefixes 'anti-', 'trans-', and very soon also 'post-' as the ultimate marker of the quintessentially modern belief in historical acceleration.[2]

1 The term 'neokantianism' can be dated to 1875, whereas 'neoplatonism' emerged in German eighteenth-century histories of philosophy, by way of a slow and intricate contraction from 'newer platonians (Neuere Platoniker)'. See Helmut Holzhey, 'Neukantianismus' and Helmut Meinhardt, 'Neuplatonismus', in *Historisches Wörterbuch der Philosophie*, ed. by Joachim Ritter, Karlfried Gründer, and Gottfried Gabriel, 13 vols (Basel: Schwabe, 1971–2007), VI (1984), pp. 747–54, 754–56.

2 The OED dates the first occurrence of 'post-Impressionist' and 'post-Impressionism' to 1910, *OED Online* (Oxford: Oxford University Press, 2000–) <http://www.oed.com> [accessed 3 January 2018].

Yet the work of theory seems to avail itself of more refined or better camouflaged prefixes, less explicitly denoting a position, historical or otherwise, and marked by operational pervasiveness rather than thematic exposition. In these prefixations, the latinate stratum of the English lexicon is heavily favoured; and latinate prefixes in particular — such as 'de-' and 're-' — boast a morphological fecundity that allows them to colonize non-latinate parts of the lexicon as well, pleasantly tingeing scholarly discourses with the latinate hue of learnedness.

Critics have begun to pay attention to the different valences these subtler prefixes bring into play in a rather underhanded fashion. Thus, Rita Felski, in her 2015 manifesto *The Limits of Critique*, switches into italics to describe a veritable war of prefixes:

> *We shortchange the significance of art by focusing on the 'de' prefix (its power to demystify, destabilize, denaturalize) at the expense of the 're' prefix: its ability to recontextualize, reconfigure, or recharge perception.*[3]

The exclamation is remarkable not just because what is being advocated for so vigorously is nothing more than a two-letter prefix, but for the way in which it mobilizes the ambiguity of the possessive pronoun 'its' to drain the supposed 'significance of art' into the antagonism of 'powerful' prefixes, detaining the detrimental 'de-' in brackets, wholeheartedly embracing the benign 're-' with a colon. Felski's poignant question — what's in a prefix? — casts itself as a

3 Rita Felski, *The Limits of Critique* (Chicago: University of Chicago Press, 2015), p. 17. Felski's book has been widely discussed. See, for example, the eight responses collected in 'On Rita Felski's *The Limits of Critique*', *PMLA*, 132.2 (March 2017), pp. 331–83, as well as Felski's response to them: 'Response', ibid., pp. 384–91.

synthesis of her masterful snapshot of current theorizing, anchored in a nuanced appreciation of the impact affect theory has had in many overlapping fields, but in particular in queer theory (which, in turn, assumed a vehicular function in the affective turns of various disciplines). Her observations that the prefix 'de-', while engendering formidably complex readings, reduces the valuable possibilities of art and politics to their 'againstness' and 'resistance' and that it frequently feigns a kind of surgical precision, a neutral negativity, are indeed compelling. Yet they also risk veiling their own detachments and the inherently unstable proximity of 'repair' and re-doubled negativity, which Eve Kosofsky Sedgwick's seminal essay playfully evokes in its subtitle 'You're So Paranoid You Probably Think This Essay Is About You'.[4] Somewhat vexingly, Felski's 'suspicions' about the use of the 'de-' prefix proves indeed more illuminating than her confidence in the power of 're-' to conclusively depart from the routines of 'critical idioms', the paralyzing stance of a hermeneutics of suspicion, the probing pointlessness of close reading, or the reflexes of ideology critique. The burden is considerable: for Felski — but she is far from alone in this — 're-' will not only reorient the humanities, but bridge the divide between the scholarly treatment of art and the layperson's appreciation, and the even more worrying rift between theory and activism within feminism and queer movements.

In a subsequent publication, a stunning essay collec-

4 Eve Kosofsky Sedgwick, 'Paranoid Reading and Reparative Reading, or, You're So Paranoid, You Probably Think This Essay Is About You', in Sedgwick, *Touching Feeling: Affect, Pedagogy, Performativity* (Durham, NC: Duke University Press, 2003), pp. 123–51. See Heather Love, 'Truth and Consequences: On Paranoid Reading and Reparative Reading', *Criticism*, 52.2 (Spring 2010), pp. 235-41, for a distinctly un-Manichaean reading of Sedgwick's essay.

tion entitled *Critique and Postcritique,* Felski and her co-editor Elizabeth Anker toned down the celebration of 're-', settling, at the very outset of their introduction, on a very even-handed re-word, though it is still being played against the chosen prefix of theories past:

> We are currently in the midst of a recalibration of thought and practice whose consequences are difficult to predict. There is little doubt that debates about the merits of critique are very much in the air and that the intellectual or political payoff of interrogating, demystifying, and defamiliarizing is no longer quite so self-evident.[5]

The very circumspect introduction acknowledges the 'complex temporality' of the totemistic 'post-' suspended in the volume's title and generated by the attempt to look for a 'postcritique' that would avoid both being uncritical, but also sliding back into critique by engaging in a 'critique of critique'.[6] The difference between 'recalibration' and the meatier 're-'words heralded in the earlier publication signals the richness of 're-', its indeed quite unpredictable, at times positively erratic behaviour. The same, of course, could be said about 'de-', even if it may have been favoured in the past, as Felski astutely observes, because it seemed to offer a clear orientation, a clear pathway to negation. The two prefixes as well as their relation have indeed always been more complicated. Gilles Deleuze's and Félix Guattari's play of 'deterritorialization' and 'reterritorialization', for example, is non-dialectic and non-antagonistic, yet gives the 're-' little chance to shine

5 Elizabeth S. Anker and Rita Felski, 'Introduction', in *Critique and Postcritique,* ed. by Anker and Felski (Durham, NC: Duke University Press, 2017), pp. 1–28 (p. 1).

6 Ibid., pp. 1, 2.

even if the 'de-' is encompassed by other re-words, such as Deleuze's understanding of repetition; and anyone who wanted to relate Jacques Derrida's 'deconstruction' to 'reconstruction' immediately revealed themselves to be a retrograde ignoramus.[7]

This is indeed the zone where the subtle fixations of prefixation tangle with the Eurocentring totems of periodization, 'neo-', 'post-', and 'anti-', all of which are preceded by the strange anachronizing gyrations of that modern master-re-signifier 'renaissance'.[8] And conversely, the story of 'de-' would have to be tracked back, at least, to Max Weber's definition of modernity as a 'disenchantment (Entzauberung)', which in turn was designed to shift away from Karl Marx's 'Entfremdung (alienation, or, literally and vexingly, de-alienation)'. Indeed, not only does Weber's term resonate in Felski's critique 'demystification', but her trenchant critique of 'de-'words strictly aligns with a grotesque de-lirium of Carl Schmitt's:

> All de-theologisations, de-politicisations, de-juridifications, de-ideologisations, de-historicisations, or any other series of de-prefixed entities [Ent-Entungen] tending towards a tabula rasa are nullified. The *tabula rasa* de-tabularises itself and is erased with its *tabula*.[9]

---

7 Adrian Parr, 'Deterritorialization/Reterritorialization' and 'Repetition', in *The Deleuze Dictionary*, revised edn, ed. by Parr (Edinburgh: Edinburgh University Press, 2010), pp. 69–72 and 225–26. Jacques Derrida, 'Letter to a Japanese Friend', trans. by David Wood and Andrew Benjamin, in *Derrida, Psyché: Inventions of the Other II*, ed. by Peggy Kamuf and Elizabeth Rottenberg (Stanford: Stanford University Press, 2008), pp. 1–6.

8 The full 'anachronic' potential of the renaissance is unlocked dazzlingly in Alexander Nagel and Christopher S. Wood, *Anachronic Renaissance* (New York: Zone Books, 2010).

9 Carl Schmitt, *Politische Theologie II: Die Legende von der Erledigung jeder Politischen Theologie* (Berlin: Duncker & Humblot, 1970), p. 124,

It should thus be clear that the prefix 're-' should be pitched against 'de-' only with the greatest care and without smoothing over its rifts or gathering its folds, and without hoisting a prefix into the dubious realm of the concept.[10] Felski's and Anker's 'recalibration' exercises this care, taking distance from anything like a *restitutio ad integrum.*[11] Yet the careful withdrawal into a recalibrative use of the prefix still does not acknowledge the plurivectorial tension that constitutes 're-', a tension that renders 're-' inescapably multistable, suited indeed for de/constituting wholes and bringing out their errant underpinnings.[12] That the divergences of language and logic can be traced perhaps at the level of the former's morphology, perhaps even more instructively than in the no less uneasy relation between syntax and predication, has been pointed out by Willard Van Orman Quine, in his terse essay on 'Prefixes':

---

in English as *Political Theology II: The Myth of the Closure of Any Political Theology*, trans. and introduced by Michael Hoelzl and Graham Ward (Cambridge: Polity, 2008), p. 128.

10 A fascinating suggestion by Edgar Morin redeemed not only by its totalizing abandon, but also by its entangling of prefixations with conceptual, 'de-'-related tensions between physics and biology, opposing 're-' to linear, mechanical determination and embedding it in the irreversible time of entropic decomposition. Cf. 'RE: From Prefix to Paradigm', *World Futures*, 61 (2005), pp. 254–67 (p. 255): '[W]e must think of RE not as a prefix but as a paradigmatic concept that informs all our thinking.'

11 As difficult as it may be to resist the lure of a title such as Robert Coyle, *'RE': God's Favorite Prefix* (Montgomery, AL: E-BookTime, 2013).

12 Alluding here to a series of ICI Publications is not to suggest that there is anything linear, let alone necessary, in the sequence of ICI projects and publications. Cf. *Tension/Spannung*, ed. by Christoph F. E. Holzhey (Vienna: Turia + Kant, 2010), *Multistable Figures: On the Critical Potentials of Ir/Reversible Aspect-Seeing*, ed. by Christoph F. E. Holzhey (Vienna: Turia + Kant, 2014), *De/Constituting Wholes: Towards Partiality Without Parts*, ed. by Manuele Gragnolati and Christoph F. E. Holzhey (Vienna: Turia + Kant, 2017).

> Our prefix re- [...] is Latin in origin and double in meaning. It can mean 'again', as in recreate and reiterate, and it can mean 'back', as in rebound. The full form is red-, and the d is kept before vowels; thus redeem (red plus emere, 'buy back') and redintegrate. In French the two senses tend to be distinguished by the vowel: re- for 'again' and ré- for 'back'. This could help us remember which words have re- and which ré-, but regrettably it is not dependable.[13]

Lack of dependability means something very different to logicians and to linguists, and the latter would no doubt add that Quine is mistaken in thinking that even the 're-'s of his English examples had the same vowels — the 're-'s of English vary, at least phonetically, between /ri/, /rɪ/, and /rə/, and /re/. A morphological segmentation of 'refer', 'defer', for example, while it may lead to interesting etymological speculations, violates the Saussurian requirement according to which the minimal linguistic sign has to be an arbitrary, yet constant union of sound and meaning.[14]

13 Willard Van Orman Quine, 'Prefixes', in Quine, *Quiddities: An Intermittently Philosophical Dictionary* (Cambridge: Harvard University Press, 1987), pp. 162–65 (p. 164). One of the words in which 're-' signifies not a repetition but a rebounding is 'reaction'. Jean Starobinski, *Action and Reaction: The Life and Adventures of a Couple*, trans. by Sophie Hawkes (New York: Zone Books, 2003) presents a stunning history of the meteoric rise of 'reaction' from Newton's third law to political semantics and psychoanalysis. This history should be registered as a tectonic shift in the varied landscape of 're-'prefixation.

14 Sergio Scalise and Emiliano Guevara, 'The Lexicalist Approach to Word-Formation and the Notion of the Lexicon', in *Handbook of Word-Formation*, ed. by Pavol Štekauer and Rochelle Lieber (Dordrecht: Springer, 2005), pp. 147–87 (p. 157). The problem of 'bound morphs' was recognized by ancient and medieval grammarians and indeed discussed in connection with the prefix 're-'. See Vivien Law, 'The Middle Ages', in *Morphologie / Morphology: Ein internationales Handbuch zur Flexion und Wortbildung / An International Handbook on Inflection and Word-Formation*, ed. by Geert Booij, Christian Lehmann, and Joachim Mugdan, 2 vols (Berlin: DeGruyter, 2000–2004), I (2000), pp. 76–90 (pp. 83–84).

The layered realm of logical and linguistic complications, thus, calls for an exploration — this is the very wager of this glossary — that acknowledges the synchronically as well as diachronically errant constitution of unbounded languages.

The contributors of the present volume encountered the prefix 're-' not through the work of one of its champions but rather through a series of serendipitous — and hence, of course, potentially 'symptomatic' — accidents and convergences. All the authors were members of a research group assembled at the ICI Berlin in 2016 in order to pursue a common two-year project entitled 'ERRANS, in Time'. While their individual projects related to the idea of an errant dimension within time and among non-synchronizable temporal experiences, their approaches, anchored in radically different disciplinary and other traditions, had not been chosen to harmonize with one another. Nonetheless, very early on, the prefix 're-' emerged in several of the individual and collaborative projects and subsequently in some of the public events organized by the ICI Fellows, from a conference on repetition in medieval culture entitled 'The Shape of Return'[15] to an engagement with 'reenactment' as a crucial strategy of contemporary art production.[16]

In the Fall of 2017, the research group presented its reflections in a public workshop adhering to a set of strict

15 'The Shape of Return: Progress, Process, and Repetition in Medieval Culture', organized by Francesco Giusti and Daniel Reeve, ICI Berlin, 29–30 September 2017 <https://www.ici-berlin.org/events/the-shape-of-return/> [accessed 3 January 2019].

16 'Over and Over and Over Again: Reenactment Strategies in Contemporary Art and Theory', organized by Cristina Baldacci, Clio Nicastro, and Arianna Sforzini, ICI Berlin, 16–17 November 2017 <https://www.ici-berlin.org/events/over-and-over/> [accessed 3 January 2019].

rules: Each participant was to give two ten-minute presentations, each dealing with a single 're-'word, one in a morning session, the other in the afternoon. The great success of the workshop inspired the idea of the current volume, which translates a sequential event into the spatial distribution of a glossary of 're-'words, far from comprehensive and proceeding not from fixed ideas about a definite meaning, let alone inherent virtue of the prefix. It registers the irreducibly plural constitutions and effects of 're-'words in order to trace the complex temporal logic folded into many of them. This requires also a return to older modes of theorizing, which, despite their 'de-'saturated terminologies, have been redescribed as efforts to emancipate repetition and reiteration from sameness — thereby sourcing ERRANS in time. The endeavour is deliberately col-lective, instigating a swarm-like exploration of very different segments and crevices of a very much erratically constituted stock of 're-'words. As such, it invites non-linear and transversal readings, but also future extensions, contestations, and re-distributions.

ARND WEDEMEYER
CHRISTOPH F. E. HOLZHEY

Recherche I

JULIE GAILLARD

According to the logical axis of time — the sequential time of the clock — the movement of 'research' (*recherche*) is always a movement forward, insofar as it is intentionally oriented toward a goal. Whether the search is oriented toward an object lost in the past or an object that is still to be discovered or invented in the future, whether the researcher knows what they are searching for or not is of no importance regarding the temporal directionality of the action denoted by this verb: one (re)searches always forward. Accordingly, both in English and in French, the prefix 're-' has a strictly intensive value: iterative usages, where 'to re-search' or '*rechercher*' means 'to search again', are quite rare and always colloquial.

At first sight, the title of Marcel Proust's famous novel, *À la recherche du temps perdu* (*In Search of Lost Time*) introduces a disturbance in this directionality of the arrow of time. The object of the search, of the '*recherche*', is 'lost time': something that should be retrieved, resuscitated. But because this object is time itself, the title is of course paradoxical, since it implies that what is searched for in a movement oriented forward in the axis of sequential time is something that is by definition irretrievable according to the very same understanding of time as infinite succession from past to future.

Two distinct translations of Proust's title exist in English. Up until a revised translation was published in 1992, the novel was known to the Anglophone readership since its first translation by C. K. Scott Moncrieff as *Remembrance of Things Past,* a phrase borrowed from Shakespeare's sonnet 30.[1] While Scott Moncrieff's translation of the text has been widely acclaimed, his rendition of the title is misleading. Proust himself complained to his French editor about this misinterpretation,[2] which indeed does away with the intensive value of 'research', occludes the intentional duality according to which time lost will be 'regained', and gears the entire project towards the resurrection of past memories. The revised, more literal translation (*In Search of Lost Time*) adequately captures the forward directionality of the search, as well as its seeming paradox with respect to linear time. But because of the constraints of the English language, it cannot fully capture two essential nuances. '*Temps perdu*', in French, is time lost,

1 Charles Kenneth Scott Moncrieff translated the first six volumes of *À la recherche du temps perdu* between 1922 and 1930. Presented as the first volume of a novel whose title was already translated as *Remembrance of Things Past, Swann's Way* was therefore published at a time when three volumes still remained to be published in French, i.e., when the final revelation of 'time regained' and the temporal structure of the whole novel had not yet been disclosed to a readership unaware of the author's design. The title has been rectified by D. J. Enright in a revised translation taking into account the second Pléiade edition of the French text published in 1987–89.

2 See Jean-Yves Tadié, *Marcel Proust. Biographie*, 2 vols (Paris: Gallimard, 1996), II, p. 478.

but also time wasted: while lost time is a metaphor of the past, time can be wasted in past, present, or future. In the French syntagma '*À la recherche du temps perdu*', this ambiguity is brought into a productive resonance with the prefix 're-'. Everything happens indeed as if the double meaning of '*temps perdu*' bounced back to reactivate the iterative dimension of the prefix 're-', now divided into two co-existing yet contradictory meanings and directions, *at the same time* intensive and iterative, forward and backward. Proust embeds the temporal eeriness of his entire novel within the enigmatic closure of a syllepsis that also opens unto a logical nightmare. What if the originality and extraordinary complexity of Proust's prolific endeavour was actually encapsulated in this two-letters prefix: 're-'? What if this coexistence of the intensive value of the prefix ghosted by a reactivated iterative value sufficed to frame the temporal paradoxes of this seven-volume masterpiece, and, indeed, the very nature of artistic creation?

The general features of the temporal paradoxes that inform Proust's novel are, of course, widely known. In the very last volume of the novel, the narrator discovers his vocation as a writer: he will write the novel that we just read. One discovers at the end how and why one must begin. That revelation occurs in the wake of a series of involuntary states that unsettle the time of the clock — states of which involuntary memory, epitomized in the Madeleine episode, is of course the most famous and most widely commented instance. The adult narrator takes a bite of a Petite Madeleine soaked in tea. He is suddenly overwhelmed by a delicious sensation of pleasure that does not seem to have an immediate or tangible cause, and that momentarily interrupts the course of life. The narrator starts to search for the cause and meaning of this eerie sensation, and, just as suddenly as the unexplainable sensation had unsettled him, the childhood memory to which this taste refers appears to him.[3] The present sensation has awoken in the narrator the memory of a past, forgotten sensation, which appears from the depth of night with the character of a vibrant and sensory certainty, and, as it were, presents the past again, 'like a stage set',[4] as a *scene*, offered to his joyful contemplation. No act of voluntary memory would have been able to reconstruct such a past in its sensory vivacity and presence. Proust devotes many pages to search for the deeper meaning of such scenes emerging from the involuntary collision of a past and a present sensation, until the narrator, in the final revelation, realizes that this bringing together of one quality common to two distinct sensations allows to abstract their common essence outside of the contingencies of time and succession, and to produce pure time. Life had produced such random moments of truth, art can also produce them by way of style.[5]

But then again, what motivates this *recherche* and keeps it in motion? Is it the appeal of its end? Or the initial momentum of its beginning? Is it possible that these are one and the same? Because of the structure of the book, and because the action of searching seems to be a voluntary action that also focuses on events presented by involuntary actions of the faculties, the *recherche* (as the eponymous

---

3 Marcel Proust, *In Search of Lost Time*, 6 vols, trans. by C. K. Scott Moncrieff and Terence Kilmartin, rev. by D. J. Enright (New York: Modern Library, 1992), I: *Swann's Way*, p. 63.

4 Ibid., p. 64. 'comme un décor de théâtre', in *À la recherche du temps perdu*, 7 vols, ed. by Jean-Yves Tadié and others (Paris: Gallimard, 1988–90), I: *Du côté de chez Swann* (1988), p. 47.

5 See Marcel Proust, *À la recherche du temps perdu*, 7 vols, ed. by Jean-Yves Tadié and others (Paris: Gallimard, 1988–90), VII: *Le Temps retrouvé* (1989), p. 196.

action of searching that gears the book according to certain directionalities) could imply both a motion *forward* of a search that, at its end, discovers that the narrator's life has been following a destiny, *and* also this movement *backward* towards past sensations and scenes that have been lost, forgotten, or repressed and would potentially hold the key to the source and meaning of the entire endeavour. This opposition between possible interpretations of the directionality of the search is widely reflected in Proustian criticism, within which general patterns can be outlined schematically according to the privileging of a retrogredient (or deterministic) hypothesis or a progredient (or teleological) hypothesis. But is it possible to imagine a third hypothesis that would synthesize and complicate the two? Before exploring this possibility of a hypothesis *a fine ad initium* in my other contribution to this volume, I shall briefly observe some of the core arguments that generally inform the criticism based on the first two hypotheses.

The retrogredient or deterministic hypothesis is most commonly represented in psychoanalytic readings, which see the novel as polarized by past events. In this hypothesis, the origin of the search is to be found in the 'lost time' of childhood crystallized in screen memories or primal scenes, which have usually been interpreted according to Oedipal models.[6] In one of the most exhaustive and com-

6 Most readings indeed agree that the Madeleine scene is a screen memory indicating the repression of a fantasy of maternal incest. See Serge Doubrovsky, *La Place de la madeleine. Ecriture et fantasme chez Proust* (Grenoble: ELLUG, 2000). See also Jean-Yves Tadié, *Le Lac inconnu. Entre Proust et Freud* (Paris: Gallimard, 2012), pp. 74–81 on screen memories and p. 90, where the author reads in the goodnight kiss scene a link with an archaic bond with the mother's breast. In an article titled 'Proustiens, encore un effort…! La déconstruction de l'inceste maternel dans *À la recherche du temps perdu*' (*French Forum*, 31.3 (Fall 2006), pp. 77–96), Giuseppina Mecchia proposes to

pelling psychoanalytic readings of the novel, Julia Kristeva, for instance, demonstrates clearly that the sequence encompassing Mamma's goodnight kiss and the Madeleine, at the very beginning of *Swann's Way*, encrypts a repressed desire for maternal incest.[7] She argues that the source for involuntary memory seems to be the underlying conflict with the maternal imago, and equates involuntary memory with unconscious memory.[8] Kristeva sees in the osmotic bond of the narrator with the mother a relation that is traumatic in nature.[9] Because traces of this traumatic bond are instantiated in scenes that keep recurring throughout the book, across the series of the narrator's love objects, across the new rooms where the grown-up will have to go to bed without the comfort of a kiss, one can indeed consider that *La Recherche* is oriented according to and toward this primal origin.

Yet Kristeva also goes beyond most psychoanalytic readings of Proust by considering not only the content of these scenes — be it manifest, latent, or intertextual — but also the very style and language in which these scenes are written. Style is the locus of what she calls, after Proust, a trans-substantiation:[10] that is, the operation

de-pathologize the relation of the narrator to the maternal figure by resorting to Deleuze and Guattari's famous 'anti-oedipal' claims. While she mobilizes the notion of an intensive, non-personal, pre-oedipal regime of desire to contend that the *Recherche* destroys the myth of incest as tragic destiny, the incestual framework and its originary character are altogether not called into question.

7 Julia Kristeva, *Le Temps sensible. Proust et l'expérience littéraire* (Paris: Gallimard, 2000), pp. 14–46.

8 Julia Kristeva, 'Entretien: La Transsubstanciation de Proust: une suspension du refoulement', in *Marcel Proust, visiteur des psychanalystes*, ed. by Andrée Bauduin and Françoise Coblenc (Paris: PUF, 2003), pp. 63–95 (p. 66).

9 Kristeva, 'Transsubstanciation de Proust', pp. 65 and 67.

10 See Kristeva, *Temps sensible*, p. 46; Kristeva, 'Transsubstanciation de Proust'.

through which signifiers are transfigured through their immersion in the drives, in order to reach essences. Beyond the unconscious, she even identifies a Schopenhauerian ambition to escape subjectivity and reach a pre-psychical state.[11] This attempt to go beyond any kind of representation is still interpreted as an attempt to overcome the trauma of separation. Psychoanalytic readings generally locate the source, the *impetus* of the search in past events that continue to shape the present, in primal scenes that must be deciphered, and are therefore predominantly deterministic.

A progredient hypothesis takes the opposite view and interprets the *Recherche* as the narrative of an apprenticeship and tale of a vocation, entirely turned forward, according to a teleology that will culminate in its last volume, when the stages of life reveal themselves as steps toward the accomplishment of a destiny. That hypothesis has been most famously formulated by Deleuze, who provocatively contended that the unity of Proust's novel does not lie in the exploration of memories of the past, but in the narrative of an apprenticeship. In the very first paragraphs of *Proust and Signs*, Deleuze states:

> On the one hand, the Search is not simply an effort to recall, an exploration of memory: search, *recherche*, is to be taken in the strong sense of the term, as we say 'the search for truth.' [...] [M]emory intervenes as a means of search, of investigation, but not the most profound means; and time past intervenes as a structure of time, but not the most profound structure. In Proust, the steeples of Martinville and Vinteuil's little phrase, which cause no memory, no resurrection of the past to intervene, will always prevail over the Madeleine and the

11 Kristeva, 'Transsubstanciation de Proust', pp. 67–68.

> cobblestones of Venice, which depend on memory and thereby still refer to a 'material explanation'.[12]

According to this hypothesis, the entire novel unfolds as an apprenticeship of signs of various natures, which one learns to decipher, thereby progressing from mundane and amorous signs towards a greater knowledge of truth, which only gives itself in art. Deleuze argues that involuntary memory plays an important, yet secondary role in this progression: reminiscences are signs that must be deciphered, and deciphering them prepares us to the plenitude of aesthetic ideas. Such contemplation, connecting the subject with the pure time of essences beyond any empirical temporality, can only be reached by way of the superior signs of art.[13] Deleuze indeed identifies four distinct structures of time. Time lost and time regained are each subdivided into two distinct types. Within time lost, there is the time that passes (the time of the clock, which one can measure differentially between two states of the same being), and there is also the time we waste (for instance, in loving someone who is not our type). Within time regained, there is, on the one hand, the time regained within time lost: for instance, the sudden affective realization, given through involuntary memory, just as the narrator bends over to unbutton his boot, that the grandmother is dead. Yet there is also a last kind of time, an originary and absolute time, that of a true eternity, that admittedly goes beyond any experiential dimensions of time, but which Deleuze recognizes as their principle, and which only gives itself through the signs of

12 Gilles Deleuze, *Proust and Signs*, trans. by Richard Howard (London: Continuum, 2008), p. 3; *Proust et les Signes* (Paris: PUF, 1964), pp. 9–10.

13 See ibid., pp. 4–9.

art.[14] While that time is not accessible through the sensuous signs, those are nonetheless necessary: for '[o]ur apprenticeship would never find its realization in art if it did not pass through those signs that give us a foretaste of time regained, and prepare us for the fulfilment of aesthetic ideas. But they do nothing more than prepare us: a mere beginning.'[15] Sensuous signs serve a crucial propaedeutic function in the trajectory that will lead to the final understanding of the true vocation and give access to the pure time of ideal essences beyond material signs. They are steps in an apprenticeship that reveals in the end its teleological nature. The time of essences is, to some extent, at stake in involuntary memory, yet only in an opaque fashion, since it is always embodied as a local essence: the Madeleine gives us Combray, the cobblestones give us Venice, etc. Even if these scenes do not give us the real Combray but rather Combray as it should have been, in an essential form detached from both past and present, its essence is nonetheless differential: its truth lies in the intertwining of a worldly, local scene and an ideal, abstract essence.[16] On the contrary, the time regained in the work of art is a primordial time, beyond experience, which is deployed neither in space, nor in succession: it is time pure and immemorial.

While Kristeva and Deleuze lead their respective enquiries in opposite directions, both reach the conclusion that the Time ultimately at stake in *À la recherche du temps perdu* is a pure time beyond empirical time, a pure time whose underlying structure is discovered at the end of the search/*recherche*. The question remains whether the immemorial time of the unconscious, identified by Kristeva

14 See ibid., pp. 12–17.
15 Ibid., p. 35.
16 Ibid., p. 40.

as the determining impetus of the *recherche,* and the immemorial time of essences, identified by Deleuze as its underlying teleological structure, can be reconciled.

If the hypothesis of the unconscious indeed implies a *backward* directionality of the *Recherche,* and if inversely the hypothesis of pure, immemorial time really directs it *forward,* then neither of these hypotheses can account for the paradox of 're-'. The beginning of this essay considered the way in which the double syllepsis structuring the French title enclosed a logical nightmare, preventing any stable interpretation: one cannot decide, among all the possible directional combinations, whether 're-' is intensive or iterative, orients itself along the flow of time or against it. By giving pre-eminence to one of the directions, one runs the risk of missing the fact that Proust does not orient his novel according to one or the other polarity of the arrow of time: rather, he troubles the poles, sets the compass frantically spinning, and makes the breaking of the arrow the preamble for its artistic re-creation.

Recherche II

Anamnesis

JULIE GAILLARD

Two meanings of the prefix 're-' coexist in the title *À la recherche du temps perdu.*[1] The *Recherche* unfolds at the same time *backward* in an iterative movement and *forward* in an intensive gesture. The (perhaps too) schematic outline of two general directional trends reveals that depending on which pole of the axis of chronological time is being given precedence, the *Recherche* can be accounted for as memory or as apprenticeship, as the narrative of a destiny determined by the workings of the unconscious or as a movement teleologically oriented toward the final revelation of a pure time of essences. Yet the double syllepsis that shapes the title suggests that the poles of such alternatives, however exclusive their directionalities might seem, would have to be thought jointly. I propose to interrogate anew this seeming incompossibility by way of a linguistic

1 See Gaillard, 'Recherche I', in this volume.

subterfuge: reframing the enquiry of 're-' by way of its Greek counterpart 'ana-', I will complicate our *recherche* on the temporality of the *Recherche* (of any *recherche*?) by confronting it to *anamnesis* — and more specifically to Jean-François Lyotard's elaboration of this notion.

'Anamnesis' is the key operator that allows Lyotard to draw an analogy between the ways in which literature and psychoanalysis, respectively, relate to time, and to define both as a *recherche du temps perdu* — as a search for lost time.[2] Even though Lyotard never devoted a full length essay to Proust's novel, the question of *temps perdu* and the strange modalities of its *recherche* haunt the philosopher's writings after his 1983 monograph *The Differend*. Indeed, they resurface systematically each time that Lyotard attempts to compare the work of psychoanalysis and the work of art (and ultimately that of philosophy) with respect to the question of the immemorial. But assimilating Proust's *Recherche* to the movement of anamnesis (literally: the action of recalling past events) by no means amounts to accrediting a determinist hypothesis according to which the directionality of the *Recherche* would be entirely geared towards a 'remembrance of things past'. On the contrary: to Lyotard, 'things past are remembered ahead' (*Le temps perdu se recherche en avant*).[3] 'Ahead', or forward: this direction does not merely describe a linear progression of the act of searching. As we shall see, this 'search ahead' rather characterizes an unsettling of sequen-

2 See Anne Tomiche, 'Anamnesis', in *Traversals of Affect: On Jean-François Lyotard*, ed. by Julie Gaillard, Claire Nouvet, and Mark Stoholski (London: Bloomsbury, 2016), pp. 73–88 (pp. 82–84).

3 Jean-François Lyotard, '*Domus* and the Megalopolis', in *The Inhuman: Reflections on Time*, transl. by Geoffrey Bennington and Rachel Bowlby (Cambridge: Polity, 1991), pp. 191–204 (p. 198); '*Domus* et la mégapole', in *L'Inhumain. Causeries sur le temps* (Paris: Klincksiesck, 2014), pp. 181–92 (p. 187).

tial time, in which the past is not recalled but actually occurs at the end of a search that it nonetheless drives forward from the beginning. By conflating '*recherche*' and 'anamnesis', Lyotard complicates the chronology that orients time in a linear succession of causes and effects from an origin to an end.

My aim is to highlight the consequences that Lyotard's assimilation of psychoanalysis and literature as *recherche du temps perdu* have in both fields: on the one hand, the temporal structure of the *Recherche* complicates a simple understanding of anamnesis as remembering or tracing back, which Lyotard challenges in order to propose a radical view of the unconscious, absolutely devoid of any representational character. On the other hand, Lyotard's conceptualization of the mechanisms of the *après-coup* allows for a renewed reading of Proust that seems to synthesize the two opposing trends — deterministic versus teleological — sketched out in my other contribution to this volume.

As Anne Tomiche has pointed out, '[Lyotard's] use of the term "anamnesis" does not refer to Plato's epistemological and psychological theory of knowledge', but is elaborated in dialogue with Freudian psychoanalysis.[4] Lyotard associates anamnesis with the Freudian *Durcharbeitung* (working-through), most famously defined in contradistinction to other modes of recollection in Freud's 1914 essay on psychoanalytic technique titled '*Erinnern, Wiederholen und Durcharbeiten* (Remembering, Repeating and Working-Through)'.[5] While something 'simply' for-

4 Tomiche, 'Anamnesis', p. 75 and p. 82.

5 Sigmund Freud, *Gesammelte Werke*, 17 vols (London: Imago, 1940–52), x: *Werke aus den Jahren 1913–1917* (1946), pp. 125–36; *The Standard Edition of the Complete Psychological Works of Sigmund Freud*, ed. and trans. by James Strachey, 24 vols (London: Hogarth, 1953–74),

gotten can be remembered, repressed 'impressions, scenes or experiences'[6] usually do not resurface as a memory, but, unbeknownst to the analysand, as an acting out in their life or in the transferential relation to the analyst. Acting-out, another name for repetition, therefore constitutes a form of resistance to remembering: stuck in the loop of reiteration, the analysand does not know what they repeat. The analytic technique, relying on free association and transference, implies a working-through of the patient's resistances, including screen memories and primal scenes, which do not 'hide' other memories but indicate the existence of repressed phantasies and mnesic traces left by impressions that have never reached consciousness.[7] Recollection, remembrance, (secondary) repression, resurfacing, repetition, resistance: all these modalities of memory imply the reiteration, indeed, the ceaseless retelling of a psyche to safeguard the linearity of causal temporality.

Lyotard's originality with respect to the Freudian *Durcharbeitung* concerns most clearly its temporal dimension.[8] Indeed, in order to elaborate anamnesis as a pivotal operator, Lyotard combines the working-through of the paper on analytic technique with the temporal structure of afterwardsness (or *Nachträglichkeit*; in French: *après-coup*) and its corollary of primal repression that Freud first described in the early *Project for a Scientific*

XII: *The Case of Schreber, Papers on Technique and Other Works* (1958), pp. 145–56. Anne Tomiche notes that 'the term [...] does not belong to Freud's main lexicon', but becomes an important operator in Lyotard's works ('Anamnesis', p. 76).

6 Freud, ibid., p. 148.

7 Ibid., pp. 148–49. For a comparison of the descriptions of screen memories in Proust and Freud, see in particular Jean-Yves Tadié, *Le Lac inconnu. Entre Proust et Freud* (Paris: Gallimard, 2012), pp. 79–85.

8 See Tomiche, *Anamnesis*, p. 82.

Psychology. As will become clear, this combination allows to think an unconscious that is not constituted by repressed representations, but is completely non-representational, and therefore radically escapes any philosophy of consciousness.[9] Anamnesis, understood as the act of working through representations and scenes towards the affect that knows no scene and escapes any representation, becomes for Lyotard a privileged modality of opening of a passage toward a 'past' that is lost — neither forgotten nor repressed, but indeed never inscribed in the first place.

As Lyotard demonstrates in *Heidegger and 'the jews'*, *Nachträglichkeit* implies 'a double blow that is constitutively asymmetrical'.[10] A first event strikes the psychic apparatus, but its intensity is too excessive to allow the psychic apparatus to record it, let alone assimilate it. Lyotard illustrates this mechanism through an analogy with a whistle too high-pitched to be perceived by the human ear.[11] Not recorded, this first blow nonetheless leaves an imperceptible trace, which is dubbed, after Freud, 'unconscious affect' — although, as Lyotard notes, it is not localizable 'within' the psyche.[12] Lyotard imagines this trace 'to be like a cloud of energy particles that are not subject to serial laws, that are not organized into sets

---

9 Claire Nouvet has analyzed this distinction in 'For "Emma"', in *Traversals of Affect*, ed. by J. Gaillard, C. Nouvet, and M. Stoholski, pp. 37–54 (p. 39).

10 Jean-François Lyotard, *Heidegger and 'the jews'*, transl. by Andreas Michel and Mark S. Robert (Minneapolis: University of Minnesota Press, 1990), p. 15. The pages on the mechanism of *après-coup* have already been commented in J. Gaillard, 'The Task of Thinking (in) The Postmodern Space of "The Zone"', in *Traversals of Affect*, ed. by J. Gaillard, C. Nouvet, and M. Stoholski, pp. 229–46 (pp. 234–37).

11 Lyotard, *Heidegger and 'the jews'*, p. 15.

12 See Nouvet, 'For "Emma"', p. 41.

that can be thought in terms of words or images, that do not experience any attraction at all'.[13] Because it has not been inscribed, the effect of the shock cannot be repressed: it insists beyond any word or image, beyond any representation, diffuse and inert. This is what Lyotard identifies after Freud as *Urverdrängung* (primal repression) — although it is not exactly 'repressed', for lack of prior inscription. The first blow is therefore 'a shock without affect'.[14] The second blow, conversely, is

> an affect without shock: I buy something in a store, anxiety crushes me, I flee, but nothing had really happened. The energy dispersed in the affective cloud condenses, gets organized, brings on an action, commands a flight without a 'real' motive. And it is this flight, the feeling that accompanies it, which informs consciousness *that* there is something, without being able to tell *what* it is. It indicates the *quod* but not the *quid*.[15]

The sudden surfacing of affect cannot be ascribed to any apparent cause. According to the chronology of temporalizing consciousness, the affect that surfaces as the second 'blow' merely indicates that 'there is' something, without providing any indication as to what that 'thing' may be. This affect has no representation, no content but itself. As such, the second shock is not properly *caused* by the first blow, whose effects remained 'outside the scene' of the psychic apparatus — outside of any representation, conscious or unconscious. This implies a dismantling of chronology. Indeed:

13 Lyotard, *Heidegger and 'the jews'*, p. 15.

14 Ibid., p. 16.

15 Ibid.

> This 'before' of the quod is also an 'after' of the *quid*. For whatever is now happening in the store (i.e., the terror and the flight) does not *come from* [*provient*]; it *comes back* [*revient*] from the first blow, from the shock, from the 'initial' excess that remained outside the scene, even unconscious, deposited outside representation. This is at least the Freudian (and Proustian) hypothesis. We may call this the chronologization, obtained by virtue of anamnesis, the setting into diachrony of what takes places in a time that is not diachronic, since what happened earlier is given at a later date (in analysis, in writing), and since what is later in the symptom (the second blow) occurs 'before' what happened earlier (the first blow). This chronologization of a time that is not chronological, this retrieval of a time (the first blow) that is lost because it has not had place and time in the psychic apparatus, that has not been noticed there, fulfills exactly the presumed function of a protective shield that Freud attributes to it in *Jenseits* [Lyotard is here referring to Freud's *Beyond the Pleasure Principle*, J.G.]. Narrative organization is constitutive of diachronic time, and the time that it constitutes has the effect of 'neutralizing' an 'initial' violence, of representing a presence without representation, of staging the obscene, of disassociating the past from the present, and of staging a recollection that must be a reappropriation of the improper, achronological affect.[16]

Affect occurs 'before' the 'initial' shock which has 'caused' it: never registered by consciousness, detached from its logical origin, the unconscious affect knows no causality and obeys no chronology. As Claire Nouvet writes, 'it presents itself over and over again, without ever representing itself, each time as if for the first time.'[17] Its achronic temporality undoes diachrony, interrupts it. Anamnesis thus can

16 Ibid., translation modified.

17 Nouvet, 'For "Emma"', p. 43.

be defined as the attempt to account for this unsettling achrony within a narrative organization that will establish the link between the first and the second blow, articulate the order of causes and effects within a chronological sequence of past, present, and future. The unconscious affect, a monstrosity for consciousness, is thereby forgotten in the very moment when it is 'treated', bound by the linear temporality of causal explanation. Always belated with respect to the apparition of the affect that seizes it, consciousness must reintegrate it into the causal diachrony of a sequence of scenes.[18]

In Lyotard's works, 'Proust' and his *Recherche* become the passwords summarizing the workings of this aberrant temporality, and this necessity for consciousness of 'explaining' the affect by integrating it within a causal sequence, by narrating it. Their mention is always parenthetical, appositional, analogical — as if they were transparent synonyms for 'anamnesis'. According to the temporality of afterwardsness, the affect without a cause befalls the subject '*before*' any 'reason' that could have caused it in the first place can be even searched for — since whatever event caused this affect has never been registered. Which is why the directionality of the search, of the *Recherche,* proceeds *at the same time* backward and forward (in the chronological time of conscious succession): my *recherche,* my anamnesis, is initiated by an affect whose cause actually lies ahead of me, since it is reconstructed *après-coup.* Trying to understand it, attempting to locate its source, I will always be out of step with it. I contend that this mech-

18 See also Tomiche, 'Anamnesis', p. 82 and Nouvet, 'For "Emma"', p. 42, as well as 'The Inarticulate Affect: Lyotard and Psychoanalytic Testimony', in *Minima Memoria: In the Wake of Jean-François Lyotard,* ed. by Claire Nouvet, Kent Still, and Zrinka Stahuljak (Stanford: Stanford University Press, 2007), pp. 106–22 (pp. 120–21).

anism, at stake in Lyotard's statement that 'things past are remembered ahead' (*le temps perdu se recherche en avant*), is also exactly what Proust describes in scenes such as the famous one of the Madeleine:

> Whence could it have come to me, this all-powerful joy? I sensed that it was connected with the taste of the tea and the cake, but that it infinitely transcended those savours, could not, indeed, be of the same nature. Where did it come from? What did it mean? How could I seize and apprehend it? [...] I put down the cup and examine my own mind. It alone can discover the truth. But how? What an abyss of uncertainty, whenever the mind feels overtaken by itself; when it, the seeker, is at the same time the dark region through which it must go seeking and where all its equipment will avail it nothing. Seek? More than that: create. It is face to face with something which does not yet exist, which it alone can make actual, which it alone can bring into the light of day.[19]

'Seek? [*chercher?*] More than that: create.' Proust writes it in so many words: explaining the sudden occurrence of an affect that befalls the subject 'without the notion of its cause' is not only a search backward to retrieve an origin: it is a search forward to produce it. And for Proust, as for Lyotard, the same goes for artistic creation in general, and for the structure of *À la recherche du temps perdu* in particular. As Anne Tomiche summarizes: 'Proust's cycle functions as a paradigm for the literary work of anamnesis because, Lyotard explains, the *Recherche*, which is entirely structured as a search for lost time, ends but only to open, at the end,

19 Marcel Proust, *In Search of Lost Time*, 6 vols, trans. by C. K. Scott Moncrieff and Terence Kilmartin, rev. by D. J. Enright (New York: Modern Library, 1992), I: *Swann's Way*, p. 61.

onto the time when the writing of the *Recherche* begins.'[20] Affect does not demand to be reintegrated into the diachrony of causes: but consciousness seeks to integrate it nonetheless, creating scenes and links between scenes to account for it — thereby bound to miss it over and over again. Which is why anamnesis is interminable, and why the *Recherche*, as Lyotard writes, 'ends on an acknowledgement of a debt [*une reconnaissance de dette*]', in spite of the immense effort of Proust's writing.[21] The 'lost time' that affect is remains 'lost' for consciousness, 'lost' for representation, and nonetheless keeps re-presenting itself in making itself be felt, obliquely, through the lure of scenes that are always questioned as such.[22]

But if the aim of anamnesis is to work through the resistance of matter, of representations, of 'scenes', in order to 'regain', as it were, or at least approach this 'essence of time lost', then it no longer has much to do with memory. What would be a memory of something that has never known any inscription? What does it mean to search back towards something that has never taken place?

With Proust, to create is to bear witness to the fact that 'some-thing' has been forgotten that escapes any retrieval because it escapes empirical diachrony. One could easily demonstrate throughout all aspects of the *Recherche* the in-

---

20 Tomiche, 'Anamnesis', p. 83.

21 Jean-François Lyotard, 'La Peinture, anamnèse du visible', in *Misère de la philosophie* (Paris: Galilée, 2000), pp. 97–115 (p. 104), my translation.

22 Tomiche, 'Anamnesis', p. 83: 'all memories and all representations are questioned as possible deceptions [...] Freud and Proust meet in this remembrance of things past which is the task of art — and if anamnesis is a search for lost time, it is not insofar as the time lost would be represented, or even presented, but insofar as art ensures a passage towards the essence of time lost, a "pure affect", the "pure event" of a "it happens".'

sistence of such a motif and its effects in style, as creation opens a passage toward the immemorial affect through the matter of words and sounds. The narrator of *The Captive*, to quote only one instance, notes that the unique accent of Vinteuil's music is proof of the irreducibly singular existence of the soul, and asks: 'That Song, ... where did Vinteuil learn it, hear it? Each artist seems like the citizen of an unknown fatherland, forgotten to themselves (*une patrie inconnue, oubliée de lui-même*)'.[23] To create is to remember the immemorial. Writing, as anamnesis, as *recherche*, is always belated, and always treasonous: it is bound to betray the pure occurrence of the affect that set it in motion. However, only this *recherche* can bear witness to the factuality of that *temps perdu*.

With the framing of 'time lost' according to primal repression, a psychoanalytic reading of the *Recherche* meets the question of the immemorial. It thus reaches the question left in suspense previously: that of the possible reconciliation of the immemorial time of the unconscious and the immemorial time of essences. As I have begun to show in my other contribution to this volume, Kristeva seems to hesitate when it comes to identifying the nature of the Schopenhauerian 'Being' she discerns at the core of the temporality of the *Recherche*. On the one hand, Being would be the unconscious, but she also ventures to hypothesize, beyond the unconscious, an inordinate attempt to escape any subjectivity and reach some state prior to the formation of the psychic apparatus [*'s'évader du subjectif*

23 Marcel Proust, *À la recherche du temps perdu*, 7 vols, ed. by Jean-Yves Tadié and others (Paris: Gallimard, 1988–90), v: *La prisonnière* (1989), p. 245, my translation. By positing that the singularity of an artist lies in a forgotten 'fatherland' inside the subject unbeknownst to them, Proust seems to describe an immemorial that is not abstract and/or collective but indeed singular.

pour atteindre le prépsychique']. [24] Lyotard's combination of the Freudian motifs of *Durcharbeitung* and *Nachträglichkeit* accounts for two kinds of unconscious: one formed by repressed representations, and the other void of any representional character. Can't we see, in this 'beyond' of the representational unconscious, some kinship with the unconscious affect that Lyotard associates with primal repression?

We saw that, on the other hand, Deleuze does away with the hypothesis of a directionality determined by the workings of the unconscious and considers the revelation of the pure, absolute, immemorial time of essences to be the consecration of an apprenticeship that will ultimately reveal that the immemorial was there from the beginning, enmeshed in all other temporalities that it sustains without hardly ever letting itself be felt, outside of reminiscences and of the signs of art. Yet Lyotard contends that Deleuze and psychoanalysis can be reconciled. In *Heidegger and 'the jews'*, having formulated the Freudian hypothesis of an unconscious devoid of representational formations, Lyotard explicitly builds on Deleuze's reading of Proust as he is about to introduce the specificity of *Nachträglichkeit*:

> [Deleuze] discovers in *À la recherche du temps perdu* the sort of past that interests us here, a past beyond [*en deçà*] of the forgotten, much closer to the present moment [*l'actuel*] than any past, at the same time that it is incapable of being solicited by voluntary and conscious memory — a past Deleuze says that is not past but always there.

---

24 Julia Kristeva, 'Entretien: La Transsubstanciation de Proust: une suspension du refoulement', in *Marcel Proust, visiteur des psychanalystes*, ed. by Andrée Bauduin and Françoise Coblenc (Paris: PUF, 2003), pp. 63–95 (p. 68).

> Whatever Deleuze might think of this, there is in Freud's own approach and tone a way of articulating this paradox of the immemorial.[25]

And elsewhere he states: 'The "signs" that Deleuze, in his *Proust,* comments on so well are these affects, outside of diachrony. Signs that are signed by the "reason" of the associative fabric, the thing, that writing at the same time marks and misses.'[26] The 'signs' signal towards the *quod* without *quid* of affect, of the immemorial, of the Lacanian 'thing (chose)', that insists 'unbeknownst', the trace of its present absence in representation.

The hypothesis of *recherche* as anamnesis, i.e. as a working through the scenes of secondary repression towards an affect without representation given by primal repression, which insists under representation, time lost under the present, brings together the determinist hypothesis of the unconscious and the teleological hypothesis of the immemorial. The *Recherche* is not oriented towards its origin or its end in a linear fashion, rather it spreads out into the illogical space where beginning and end correspond, where the end motivates, creates the beginning. Time lost is not a time accessible to experience yet its effects are felt concretely: it is what motivates the perpetual search, constantly torn between the two poles of an end, that is an origin, and of an origin, that comes at the end.

---

25 Lyotard, *Heidegger and 'the jews'*, p. 12, translation modified.

26 Lyotard, 'La Peinture, anamnèse du visible', p. 103, my translation; cf. 'Les "signes" que Deleuze, dans son *Proust,* commente si bien, sont ces affects, hors diachronie. Des signes que signe la "raison" du tissu associatif, la chose, que l'écriture à la fois marque et manque.'

Recirculation

The Wandering of Digital Images in Post-Internet Art

CRISTINA BALDACCI

Starting from the double meaning of circulation as 'continuous motion' and 'public availability of something', I would like to address the flow of digital images; principally the idea of *recirculation* as a process through which both visual and cultural imagery are put in motion over and over again in the current information age, and in the context of post-Internet art in particular.[1]

Recirculation has of course to do with the many ways in which images are nowadays produced and exchanged, as well as evaluated and accepted. That the accelerated dissemination of images is rapidly changing the relationship to them is already well known. More and more images affect us and, at the same time, we affect them as viewers

1 For a definition of post-Internet art, see Marisa Olson, 'Postinternet: Art After the Internet', *Foam Magazine*, 29 (2011), pp. 59–63 (p. 60).

too by repetitively circulating and framing them anew, with each Internet 'share', 'tweet', or 'meme' that makes them go viral as doppelgängers. But that makes us loose control over them both as senders and receivers. Once an image is online, it can presumably be accessed and used by almost everyone regardless of intent, thus distancing the image from the initial purpose for which it was uploaded.[2] In this regard, it is also important to remember that, theoretically, the source of a digital image is less relevant than its destination, that is, the recipient, or rather, the vast and diverse audiences it may reach.

These new modes of distribution present, no doubt, one of the main challenges for artists, since the World Wide Web permits the large diffusion of images outside institutional contexts and can have a positive effect in terms of critique and social impact. It can therefore function as an alternative approach to the traditional system of circulation — and also production of meaning —, through which artists are able to develop different strategies of resistance, although there is still a margin for doubt. The way in which images are received and operated is in fact not predictable, and, moreover, no one can really determine who the final receiver is: if it is still human or, more likely, an algorithm.[3]

2 See Marisa Olson, 'Lost Not Found: The Circulation of Images in Digital Visual Culture', in *Words Without Pictures*, ed. by Alex Klein (Los Angeles: LACMA, 2009), pp. 274–84 (pp. 276, 280).

3 I won't take into consideration here the vast and challenging debate around what Harun Farocki, in his video work *Eye/Machine I* (2000), referred to as 'operational images', and what Trevor Paglen calls 'invisible images', namely, images that don't need humans because they are made 'by machines for other machines': images that are dramatically changing our visual culture and the way in which we have to approach and study images by establishing both new categories and interpretative tools borrowed from computer science. See Trevor Paglen, 'Operational Images', *e-flux journal*, 59 (2014) <https://www.e-flux.com/journal/59/61130/

With its vast social communities that everyday spread large amounts of images across different screens and among distributed spectators all over the world, the Internet has merely augmented a process that is clearly nothing new. The circulation of images concerns a 'visual economy',[4] which in the twentieth century has been reflected upon both in the tradition of 'the wandering image', initiated by Walter Benjamin, with the new possibilities of the mechanical reproduction of images as a crucial starting-point, and Aby Warburg's account of the survival of ancient image forms, which he configures as an engram, a mnestic trace reactivated under specific circumstances or in the presence of specific stimuli.[5]

By appropriating, editing, and recirculating presumed 'originals',[6] artists act as special 'iconographers' who both

operational-images/> [accessed 18 December 2018]; and, by the same author, 'Invisible Images (Your Pictures Are Looking at You)', *The New Inquiry*, 8 December 2016 <https://thenewinquiry.com/invisible-images-your-pictures-are-looking-at-you/> [accessed 18 December 2018].

4 Significantly enough, in the last edition of her propaedeutic book on visual studies, Gillian Rose has answered the central question of what difference digital technologies are making in the understanding of the contemporary iconosphere by adding a fourth 'site' dedicated to circulation to the three previously existing ones: the site of the production of an image, the image itself, and the sites of its audiencing. See Gillian Rose, *Visual Metodologies: An Introduction to Researching with Visual Materials* (London: Sage, 2016).

5 Following his interests in empathy theory and bodily movement, Warburg further evolved the concept of engram, first coined by neurologist Richard Semon — who also referred to it as 'mneme' — into what he called 'dynamogram', that is, a visual inscription of primal, affective experiences.

6 With all the uncertainties that this notion of an 'original' includes, since originality is a problematic and rather recent concept, championed mostly by Romanticism, which the avantgarde movements have vigorously attacked. A picture is indeed a site where a variety of non-original images mix and clash, and repetition is possible not because an image

produce and consume images.[7] In so doing, they keep questioning the ontology of the image, especially in its shift from analogic to digital, which has led to various new issues related to their life and afterlife. Just to briefly name a few: (1) the question of the transferability of images, not only from one medium or support to another, but from one context to another as well; (2) the question of their alleged immateriality, considering that the way in which images get seen online is shaped by energy and algorithmic patterns; (3) the question of the difference between what is real and what is unreal when we look at images.

Hito Steyerl's theoretical writings, which together with her practice as a video artist and filmmaker represent some of the most influential thoughts in the current debate on the status and dispersion of digital images, will help me to unpack these issues.

For Steyerl, 'postproducing, launching, and accelerating' an image — that is, diffusing it — is more important than making it. The term she coined to describe this principle is 'circulationism', which, although it relates especially to our digital age, according to her emerged in a very specific moment in time: in 1989, namely when, in the midst of the Romanian uprising, 'protesters invaded TV studios to make history'. Since then — Steyerl suggests — images have changed their function and have become 'nodes of energy and matter that migrate across different supports, shaping and affecting people, landscapes, polit-

---

or gesture has a specific origin — thus could be considered unique — but simply because of its anteriority.

7 Cf. *Les Artistes iconographes/Artists as Iconographers*, ed. by Garance Chabert and Aurélien Mole (Paris: Empire Books-Villa du Parc, 2018), pp. 319–26.

ics, and social systems'.[8] And that basically means that images not only present reality, they also make it.

However, the fluidity, variability, and migration of images — in particular when artistic appropriation is involved — inevitably produce an impoverishment, if not of content, at least of form. It is in this regard that Steyerl speaks of the 'poor image', namely a copy of poor quality, of low resolution and definition,[9] which is bound to a relentless peregrination. And which ends up being 'a ghost of an image, a preview, a thumbnail, an errant idea, an itinerant image distributed for free, squeezed through slow digital connections, compressed, reproduced, ripped, remixed, as well as copied and pasted into other channels of distribution.'[10]

Once removed from secure places such as the archive and the film library, the 'poor image' is thrown into a land of uncertainty, that is, the Internet. Here it becomes available, therefore also exposed, to easy appropriation, reuse, and alteration, allowing a wider audience to participate in its new reproduction and distribution processes. Speed, intensity, and circulation become its new features; while qualities such as resolution and exchange value recede into the background, or even disappear. Though what comes back is the aura, which is no longer based on the notion

8 Cf. Hito Steyerl, 'Too Much World: Is the Internet Dead?', in *The Internet Does Not Exist*, ed. by Julieta Aranda, Brian Kuan Wood, and Anton Vidokle (Berlin: Sternberg Press, 2015), pp. 10–26 (pp. 11, 20–21).

9 On the concept of low definition see Francesco Casetti and Antonio Somaini, 'The Conflict Between High Definition and Low Definition in Contemporary Cinema', *Convergence*, 19.4 (2013), pp. 415–22; and Antonio Somaini and Andrea Pinotti, *Cultura visuale. Immagini, sguardi, media, dispositivi* (Turin: Einaudi, 2016), in particular chapter 5.

10 Cf. Hito Steyerl, 'In Defense of the Poor Image', in *The Wretched of the Screen* (Berlin: Sternberg Press, 2012), pp. 31–45 (p. 32).

of uniqueness, authenticity, and authorship, but rather — in Steyerl's words — 'on the transience of the copy'.[11]

The idea of the remediation of the image is crucial here. Granted that the original, even if reproduced as an exact copy, is never a true replica because it loses the two qualities that make it unique — the here and now —, the copy of the original gets its own aura as well, since, thanks to its refashioning, it is linked to a specific new context and time.[12]

Since in the digital visual domain things are evolving rapidly, Steyerl is at the same moment updating and reshaping her thoughts. As she argues, in the last decade (her text on the 'poor image' was first published in 2009) two main changes occurred: first, what previously would have been considered high resolution images are now very normal and diffused images; second, what once was regarded as a free circulation of images, today increasingly appears as a regulated flow, mainly under the control of powerful platforms. And, what's more, energy has turned out to be a force or medium for circulation, which affects both natural, social, and power relations, since the transmission of digital images (Steyerl refers to videos in particular) will soon be the principal cause of electricity consumption in the world. That is why she is now progressively moving from the definition of 'poor images' towards that of 'power images'.[13]

---

11 Ibid., p. 42.

12 Cf. Andrea Pinotti, 'Optic Distance, Haptic Immersion', in *The Encyclopedic Palace*, ed. by Massimiliano Gioni and Natalie Bell (Venice: La Biennale di Venezia–Marsilio, 2013), pp. 193–94; and Boris Groys, 'Art Topology: The Reproduction of Aura', in *When Attitudes Become Form: Bern 1969/Venice 2013*, ed. by Germano Celant (Milan: Fondazione Prada, 2013), pp. 451–56.

13 This is a very condensed summary of a much more articulated talk she

Allan Sekula, whose artistic work is likewise rooted in a strong theoretical basis and who produced a consistent corpus of writings throughout his entire career (he died in 2013), was even more sceptical than Steyerl is, and made similarly critical comments in relation to the photographic archive.[14] For him the image's 'loss of context' starts already from the archive tout court. 'In an archive', he writes, 'the possibility of meaning is "liberated" from the actual contingencies of use. But this liberation is also a loss, an *abstraction* from the complexity and richness of use.' This is because photographic meaning depends largely on context, which has both a spatial and temporal connotation.'[15]

The (archival) image abstraction described by Sekula — which can be compared to the (digital) image poverty pointed out by Steyerl — undermines, in his words, the 'notion of mutual recognition, of global connectedness and legibility, at the heart of the promise of the Internet', and highlights the dangers of digital iconographic greed, kleptomania, and piracy. Referring especially to digital images, in fact, Sekula warns of another main and often underestimated risk: that of the increasing privatization of images

---

recently gave in the context of the conference on *Art/Politics* at n.b.k. – Neuer Berliner Kunstverein in Berlin on 12 May 2018.

14 I won't consider here indexicality as an opposition between analogue and digital photography, since the most recent debate on this subject matter is eliminating the problem by giving a whole new interpretation to indexicality, both from a historical and contemporary perspective. For a short overview, see Jaime Schwartz, 'Is a Photograph Still an Index If It's on the Internet?', *Dis Magazine* <http://dismagazine.com/discussion/41736/a-discursive-mask/> [accessed 18 December 2018].

15 Cf. Allan Sekula, 'Reading an Archive: Photography Between Labour and Capital', in *The Photography Reader*, ed. by Liz Wells (London: Routledge, 2003), pp. 443–52 (p. 444).

or change of ownership, and the consequent monopolization of copyright.[16]

Under these circumstances, the flow and recirculation of the 'poor' images would seem to be jeopardized by private property appetites, the control exercised by search engines, and the congestion produced by the increasing amount of ghost data that accumulate on a daily basis as 'digital debris' and are dispersed as spam.[17]

But, in the end, should this only be seen as a danger? Certainly not. If on the one side poor images show the hidden social mechanisms and political forces that rule today's visual economy, on the other they also create an alternative circuit that fosters the reappearance and recirculation of excluded or marginalized visual materials, creating new networks and debates. Furthermore, as contemporary art practices show, it also facilitates the images' reenactment and refashioning, thus opening ever new, eclectic visual possibilities.

Since the circulation of poor images feeds both capitalist media appetites and alternative artistic experimentation, Steyerl reserves judgment.[18] Alongside sameness, anaesthesia, alienation, and control, the circulation of poor images also has the potential to create — according to her — 'disruptive movements of thought and affect', continu-

---

16 The target of Sekula's critique was principally the 'cybericonographic omnivore' Bill Gates who — as long as he owned the Corbis agency — collected and controlled almost every valuable image in the world, thus also their reproducibility and circulation, or better, since these are services for a fee, their 'traffic'. Cf. Allan Sekula, 'Between the Net and the Deep Blue Sea (Rethinking the Traffic in Photographs)', *October*, 102 (2002), pp. 3–34 (pp. 3, 11).

17 See Hito Steyerl, 'Digital Debris: Spam and Scam', *October*, 138 (2011), pp. 70–80.

18 Steyerl's remarks concern especially experimental cinema, hence audiovisual material.

ing, in the twenty-first century, the tradition of avant-garde 'non-conformist information circuits'. The shift of attention is thus all on the afterlife of images, on their 'swarm circulation, digital dispersion, fractured and flexible temporalities'. Which means that in the digital realm the focus is no more on the 'original' image itself (the real thing) but on the conditions of its recurrent circulation (reality) and translation.[19]

19 Cf. Steyerl, 'In Defense of the Poor Image', pp. 43–44; and also Hito Steyerl, 'Politics of the Archive: Translations in Film', *transversal* (Vienna: eipcp, 2008) <http://eipcp.net/transversal/0608/steyerl/en> [accessed 18 December 2018]; repr. in Steyerl, *Beyond Representation: Essays 1999–2009*, ed. by Marius Babias (Berlin: n.b.k., 2016), pp. 160–66.

Recitation

Lyric Time(s) I

FRANCESCO GIUSTI

The current debate on the lyric is imbued with diverse temporalities, but they are rarely explored in their multilevel interactions. What is the time of lyric writing and reading? What is the temporality of the lyric as a literary genre? How do present poems relate to past and future poems? Summarizing the formation of the modern idea of lyric in the nineteenth century in their introduction to *The Lyric Theory Reader*, Virginia Jackson and Yopie Prins write:

> If for Hegel the ideal lyric poet would move civilization forward in its perfect self-expression, for [John Stuart] Mill the ideal lyric poet would have to be the representative of both original nature and acquired culture, something no one yet had done perfectly. For such idealized accounts, the lyric poet could only be an imagined figure, a hero of a poetry yet to appear (as indeed the poet became rather explicitly

> for Ralph Waldo Emerson, until Walt Whitman volunteered for the job).[1]

This concept of the lyric, or rather of the ideal lyric project, is patently authoritarian, essentialist, and teleological. It is also quite voyeuristic, if we consider that, according to such a definition, the reader witnesses — unseen — a first person subject (precariously assimilated to the actual poet) confessing itself to itself.[2] This way the subject is observed in its autonomous self-formation and an enormous power is accredited to individual speech. Jackson and Prins, indeed, purport to show that this idea of the lyric is a creation of the nineteenth century that twentieth-century literary criticism has turned into a real, given genre rather than an ideal yet to be achieved.

By being read *as* lyric, a wide range of short verse writing has thus been *lyricized*: a historically situated interpretive frame has been inappropriately applied to a variety of poetic forms produced not only afterwards, but also in the previous centuries. The creation of such an *archigenre* is what Gérard Genette called a 'retrospective illusion'.[3] Regardless of the historical accuracy of Jackson and Prins's

---

1 *The Lyric Theory Reader. A Critical Anthology*, ed. by Virginia Jackson and Yopie Prins (Baltimore: Johns Hopkins University Press, 2014), pp. 1–8 (p. 3). See also pp. 11–16, the editors' introduction to the section 'Genre Theory'.

2 Northrop Frye echoes John Stuart Mill's declaration 'eloquence is *heard*; poetry is *over*heard' when he states that a lyric poem is 'preeminently the utterance that is overheard'. Cf. John Stuart Mill, 'What is Poetry?', *The Monthly Repository*, n.s., 7 (1833), pp. 60–70 (p. 64) and Northrop Frye, *The Anatomy of Criticism: Four Essays* (Princeton: Princeton University Press, 1957), p. 249. For T. S. Eliot, in first-person poetry, or 'meditative verse', the poet is 'talking to himself — or to nobody', 'The Three Voices of Poetry', in *On Poetry and Poets* (London: Faber and Faber, 1957), pp. 89–102 (p. 89).

3 Gérard Genette, *The Architext: An Introduction*, trans. by Jane E. Lewin (Berkeley: University of California Press, 1992) (a selection repr. in *The Lyric Theory Reader*, pp. 17–30).

analysis, I would contend that the process they outline could help define the inner workings of the lyric as a genre instead of shattering it. In other words, I argue that it is possible to historicize the post-Romantic conception without ending up with a series of entirely unrelated texts. Two and a half millennia of literary production have contributed to the shaping of the Romantic idea of lyric as much as that idea has contributed to produce poems that intend to be lyric.

Perhaps, this is my claim, the lyric itself allows for a 'retrospective illusion'.[4] One should thus look for a set of reiterated gestures[5] that could help gather together texts from different epochs and describe the lyric as a transhistorical discursive mode — rather than a historical and contextual literary genre.[6] If the process outlined by Jackson and Prins has reduced historical difference to ideal sameness, how can one recover diversity without renouncing any theoretical perspective? I want to approach the

---

4 For the retrospective definition of the lyric in ancient literary theory and its productive anachronism, see W. Ralph Johnson, *The Idea of Lyric: Lyric Modes in Ancient and Modern Poetry* (Berkeley: University of California Press, 1982), pp. 83–95.

5 For Dominique Rabaté, the poem itself is a *lyric gesture* of re-enunciation or *re-citation*, see *Gestes lyriques* (Paris: José Corti, 2013); 'Énonciation poétique, énonciation lyrique', in *Figures du sujet lyrique*, ed. by Dominique Rabaté (Paris: PUF, 1996), pp. 65–79; and 'A World of Gestures', *Journal of Literary Theory*, 11.1 (2017), special issue *Theories of Lyric*, ed. by Claudia Hillebrandt, Sonja Klimek, Ralph Müller, William Waters, and Rüdiger Zymner, pp. 89–96.

6 *Transhistorical* does not mean *meta-historical*. Instead of focusing on contextual differences, a transhistorical approach, as that pursued by Jonathan Culler in *Theory of the Lyric* (Cambridge, MA: Harvard University Press, 2015), seeks traces of historical continuity in cultural artefacts. It does not propose immutable ahistorical features, but rather traces recurrences across contextual variations. Through iteration, difference can emerge, and variations allow tracking continuity. See Francesco Giusti, 'The Lyric in Theory. A Conversation with Jonathan Culler', *Los Angeles Review of Books*, 27 May 2017.

lyric from a specific angle, namely the multilayered and asynchronous temporalities that the lyric both establishes and is constituted by. As a general key to unlock them, I shall deploy the term *recite*, from Latin *recitare* 'read aloud, repeat from memory, declaim', which is composed of *re-* 'back, again' and *citare* 'to summon'. At different moments, I shall use the word in both its senses of 'to repeat aloud' and 'to quote again'. By shedding light on this double act — the *recitation* of the poem and the *re-citation* of prior lyric gestures — correspondences between the time of the poem and the time of the genre might emerge.

In Augustine's *Confessions*, the recitation of a poem is presented as a good example of his notion of time (XI, 38):

> Imagine that I am to recite [*dicturus*] a hymn [*canticum*] that I know. Before I start, my expectation [*expectatio*] extends to the hymn as a whole. But once I begin, whatever part of that expectation I have plucked away goes into the past and is retained in my memory: the life force of my performance [*actionis*] is in tension [*distenditur*] between memory (because of what I have already spoken) and expectation (because of what I have yet to say). My awareness [*attentio*] is in the present though; and through it what was future crosses over to become the past. The longer the performance continues, the more my expectation is reduced and my memory prolonged, until expectation is entirely exhausted: and once the whole performance [*actio*] of the hymn is finished it shifts into memory.[7]

For Augustine, the recitation of a *canticum* is a suitable instance of the workings of temporality in the human mind:

7 Augustine, *Confessions*, ed. and trans. by Carolyn J.-B. Hammond, 2 vols (Cambridge, MA: Harvard University Press, 2014–16), II: pp. 253–55.

on the one hand the establishment of past and future, on the other hand the progressive subdivision of the present — from the whole poem down to the individual syllables. Both past and future are produced in the act of reading, the former as memory and the latter as expectation. As memory extends itself, so expectation is gradually reduced. The action of voicing marks the present moment that sets apart what has been already repeated from what is yet to come. At the same time, as Augustine observes, an arbitrary subdivision of the text/time delimits the extension of the present.

I do not want to enter Augustine's discussion of time here; rather I am interested in this passage as the trace of a textual practice. In the retrieval of memory, past and future have nothing to do with the acquisition or transmission of knowledge: it is posited that the reciter already knows the poem. The present is thus an action, not a reflection. In recitation, expectation does not concern unforeseeable events, but rather the anticipation of what is going to happen, or is likely to happen. In order to have expectations, the reciter (or the reader) must recognize the unfolding of a structure; in order for time to pass, the structure must be recognizable. The unexpected, one might deduce, breaks the passing of time. The deviance — the event that could not be predicted based on previously known causes — erupts as an error, a *clinamen* — in the terms of Lucretius's *De Rerum Natura* (II, 289–94) which translate the *parénklisis* of Epicurean physics. Nothing, of course, prevents one from tracing outcomes back to some anterior causes — this is probably one of the aims of retrospective narration.

I will leave aside the question of error for now, and focus instead on the temporality of reading. The present moment of reading can be established only within some kind of recursive structure — which distends itself in a system of recollections and expectations — and under the condition that the gesture is performed again. In the case of a poem, the present moment, which is an action in time, is also the re-enactment of the past: the poem already exists for the reader, just as in Augustine's example it is already in the reciter's memory.

In *The Time That Remains,* Giorgio Agamben also refers to a poem to exemplify what he defines as *messianic time*: a time that is moving towards its end, but whose end and fulfilment — the Apocalypse — are beyond time. Here Agamben connects time not to the performing reader, but to the structure of the poem itself. Expectations are not generated by prior knowledge, but by the internal organization of the text. For him,

> [t]he sestina — and, in this sense, every poem — is a soteriological device which, through the sophisticated *mēchanē* of the announcement and retrieval of rhyming end words (which correspond to typological relations between past and present), transforms chronological time into messianic time. Just as this time is not other to chronological time or eternity, but is the transformation that time undergoes when it is taken for a remnant, so too is the time of the sestina the metamorphosis that time undergoes insofar as it is the time of the end, the *time that the poem takes to come to an end.*[8]

Agamben refers specifically to the system of rhymes, but in *The End of the Poem* he seems to imply that even non-

8 Giorgio Agamben, *The Time That Remains: A Commentary on the Letter to the Romans,* trans. by Patricia Dailey (Stanford: Stanford University Press, 2005), pp. 82–83.

rhyming poems work in accordance to *messianic time*.[9] They establish their own time. This time is not something other than *chronos*; it is rather an organization of *chronos* into a *kairos* that not only moves towards its anticipated end, but is also internally structured in a system of announcements and retrievals, that is, in a system of expectations and memories. If *messianic time* marks the beginning and the end of time, thus reducing its openness, it also animates it through the repetition of rhymes, where each ending sound anticipates and recalls identical ones:

> Through this complicated to-and-fro directed forward and backward, the chronological sequence of linear homogeneous time is completely transformed into rhythmic constellations themselves in movement. It is not that there is another time, coming from who-knows-where that would substitute for chronological time; to the contrary, what we have is the same time that organizes itself through its own somewhat hidden internal pulsation, in order to make place for the time of the poem.[10]

As progressing in the poem line after line, the reader is caught in the fleeting present of enunciation in which the memory of previous words meets the expectation of the words to come.

Given that Augustine's and Agamben's exemplifications illustrate the temporality active within the poem, the question arises whether this multidirectional temporality might be operative at the level of the literary genre too. To explore this hypothesis, I shall focus in the second part of my contribution on Rilke's decision not to translate, but

9 Giorgio Agamben, 'The End of the Poem', in *The End of the Poem: Studies in Poetics*, trans. by Daniel Heller-Roazen (Stanford: Stanford University Press, 1999), pp. 109–15.

10 Agamben, *The Time That Remains*, p. 82.

rather to rewrite Dante's *Vita nova* (1293–1295) in the first of the *Duineser Elegien* (1912), and on the reasons for that suggested in the poem itself. From *recitation* in the sense of *repeating* a poem *aloud*, I shall then expand to *re-citation* in the sense of *quoting* another poem *again*. But before reaching the level of the literary genre, I shall first look at Dante's 'Tanto gentile e tanto onesta pare' ('Such sweet decorum and such gentle grace') and the ways in which this sonnet, written several years earlier, is subsequently included in the prosimetric structure of the *Vita nova*. What kind of relationship does the lyric poem establish with the surrounding narrative prose? What kind of temporality is Dante offering here for the lyric?

Robert Pogue Harrison defines 'Tanto gentile e tanto onesta pare' as the 'ideal lyric' of the *Vita nova* inasmuch as it presents a fully-fledged 'circle of incorporation', and for Manuele Gragnolati and Francesca Southerden it constitutes a 'moment of perfect plenitude'.[11] The sonnet is generally acknowledged to be the fullest embodiment of the praise (*loda*) that Dante proposes in *Vita nova* 10 (XVII–XIX) as his new poetic style.[12]

---

11 Although this is the poem in which Dante gets closest to the bodily presence of Beatrice, for Harrison the lady is still withdrawing something of herself from full revelation while at once animating the poetic voice, see Robert Pogue Harrison, *The Body of Beatrice* (Baltimore: Johns Hopkins University Press, 1988), pp. 31–46 (pp. 31 and 44). In their account of the sonnet, Gragnolati and Southerden instead think of the poem as an accomplished full revelation in an ecstatic now, 'a (temporary) leap into the instantaneity of glory, which the poem does not so much describe as actively perform', see Manuele Gragnolati and Francesca Southerden, 'Dalla perdita al possesso. Forme di temporalità non lineare nelle epifanie liriche di Cavalcanti, Dante e Petrarca', *Chroniques italiennes*, séries web 32 (1/2017), pp. 136–54 (pp. 143 and 147) <http://www.univ-paris3.fr/medias/fichier/gragnolati-southerden_1501152291404.pdf> [accessed 20 December 2018]. Translation of the authors.

12 I follow the text and the subdivision of the text into 31 paragraphs

Such sweet decorum and such gentle grace
attends my lady's greeting as she moves
that lips can only tremble into silence,
and eyes dare not attempt to gaze at her.
Moving benignly clothed in humility,
untouched by all the praise along her way,
she seems to be a creature come from Heaven
to Earth to manifest a miracle.
Miraculously gracious to behold,
her sweetness reaches, through the eyes, the heart
(who has not felt this cannot understand),
and from her lips it seems there moves a gracious
spirit, so deeply loving that it glides
into the souls of men, whispering: 'Sigh!'[13]

To understand the specific temporality of this poem, one has to pay attention to how it is embedded in the prose of paragraph 17 (XXVI) of the *Vita nova*. Indeed, the preceding narrative (*ragione*, in Dante's terms) provides the scene of enunciation that frames the lyric utterance. Before saying (*dire*) the sonnet,[14] Dante describes the wondrous appearance of Beatrice in the streets of Florence and the

---

provided in Dante Alighieri, *Vita nova*, ed. by Guglielmo Gorni (Turin: Einaudi, 1996). The corresponding section in Barbi's edition is provided in Roman numerals in parenthesis. 'Tanto gentile e tanto onesta pare / la donna mia quand'ella altrui saluta, / ch'ogne lingua deven tremando muta / e gli occhi no l'ardiscon di guardare. // Ella si va, sentendosi laudare, / benignamente d'umiltà vestuta; / e par che sia una cosa venuta / da cielo in terra a miracol mostrare. / Mostrasi sì piacente a chi la mira, / che dà per gli occhi una dolcezza al core, / che 'ntender no·lla può chi no·lla prova; / e par che della sua labbia si mova / un spirito soave pien d'amore, / che va dicendo all'anima: Sospira.' (Dante, *Vita nova*, pp. 159–61.)

13 Dante Alighieri, *Dante's* Vita Nuova. *New Edition: A Translation and an Essay*, ed. and trans. by Mark Musa (Bloomington: Indiana University Press, 1973), p. 57.

14 Although the *Vita nova* as a literary work strongly marks its being *written*, it consistently presents the production of poetry as an act of *saying* and associates it with verbs of vocalization (*dire*). This act does not expect a passive reader or listener; it is rather meant to respond to someone or to engender a variety of active responses.

effect she has on the people who hasten to see her. This is a recurrent event: Beatrice attracts and affects her beholders every time she makes an appearance in a public place. As Dante openly declares, he composes the sonnet to share Beatrice's miraculous operations with the people who cannot see her in person (but probably have heard of her). Therefore, the poem is not a representation of a prior real event to be interpreted by selected expert readers (Dante's fellow love poets), as it is the case with the sonnet 'A ciascun'alma presa e gentil core' ('To every captive soul and loving heart') in the first paragraph (III). Rather it is conceived as a verbal substitute for Beatrice that, when recited, aims to induce the same actual effects in its readers that the actual woman induces in her beholders. The poem is meant to let other people participate in the iterable advent of Beatrice.

Furthermore, the enunciation of the poem — reenacted at every recitation of the text — covers and articulates a definite time span. As we read in Dante's prose, just after Beatrice's passage, several bystanders express in words their wonder at the event and their admiration for the woman's angelic beauty. The presence of Beatrice engenders in them so strong an honesty that, during the actual event of Beatrice's appearance, they cannot but fall silent and lower their eyes. The pleasant inner experience of her manifestation is so intense that bystanders are not able to retell it, and no one could look at her without sighing upon the very first glance. No one but Dante apparently. Even though exposed to Beatrice's impact, the poet wants to say the event while it happens, before he is eventually forced to sigh too. The poem wants to make the event present to the readers while it is taking place and up to the (expected) sighing, between Beatrice's first appearance on the scene and the silence that her passing by imposes on bystanders.[15]

The crystallized moment — which encapsulates iteration — moves toward the final sigh that is the threshold to the fullness of experience and from where the poem can begin (again). The poem 'happens' after its end and before its beginning. The iterability of the poem as event is not made explicit in the poem, but only in the prose.[16] The poem, though, offers itself for repetition in different 'presents' thanks to its verbal tenses (present and gerund), the establishment of its own *kairos*, and the (shareable) open position of its speaker. Referentiality is kept open in the poem: the utterance finds its referents only in the larger world in which it takes place, in this case the fictional world created by the narrative in which it is inserted.[17] As a member of a responsive collectivity, the speaker is left relatively non-individuated since the active role is delegated to Beatrice. By inserting in the frame narrative of the *Vita nova* a poem that he had written previously, Dante identifies him-

---

15 Perhaps, in order to be able to look and speak, the speaker has to partially withdraw his presence from the scene of passing and greeting, or at least slightly delay Beatrice's effect on him. Indeed, Beatrice addresses her greeting to others (*altrui*). Of course, the narrative reason could also apply here: in paragraph 5 (X–XII), Beatrice had already denied her sweet greeting to Dante and this deprivation caused the adoption of the style of praise, which does not ask for any kind of reciprocation.

16 The notion of the poem as event shares some traits with Attridge's concept of *act-event*: the position of both activity and passivity in which the reader finds herself when responding to a text as a literary work, see Derek Attridge, *The Work of Literature* (Oxford: Oxford University Press, 2015). For Attridge, this response concerns literature in general; I am interested in the linguistic and rhetorical strategies by which the lyric enables such response.

17 In other cases, a more stable referent can be provided by our 'real' world in the context of the re-enactment of the poem, by literary history, or by paratextual or macrotextual elements, such as titles, epigraphs, or recurrent proper names (for instance, Laura in Petrarch's *Canzoniere*).

self as the author — the first person to *say* the poem — but also as a reader of the product of a creative power which lies somewhere else.[18] In other words, he is already re-enacting it.

The verbal gesture of saying or praising the beloved (or any other object of cultural value) — with no ambition to contain her in a full representation — is an act of presence as much as a quotable form. The poem is an effect of Beatrice that intends to have the same, or at least a similar, effect on its readers. Over a certain time span, the presence of the speaker is engendered by the presence of Beatrice as much as the presence of the reader is engendered (up to the conclusive sigh) by the presence of the poem.[19] One could say, following Agamben, that the fullness of experience is beyond the limits of the poem, in the silence brought about by the sigh, but the entire utterance moves toward that silence which is outside of the poem, outside of the articulation of time.

The poem is not just made of words that, when read out loud, are translated into bodily actions or bring forth what they convey as meaning, as it happens in an oath, a court sentence, or an instruction book, what could be

---

18 As at least twelve other poems included in the *Vita nova*, 'Tanto gentile e tanto onesta pare' had an attested previous circulation as a freestanding poem, see Dante Alighieri, *Rime giovanili e della* Vita nuova, ed. by Teodolinda Barolini, notes by Manuele Gragnolati (Milano: Rizzoli Bur, 2009), pp. 392–402. The subsequent transmission of the *Vita nova* shows the resistance of the lyric to be fully absorbed into the self-exegetical prose, and to a certain extent, into Dante's authorial self-projection. Boccaccio transcribes the *Vita nova*, moving Dante's analytical annotations to the poems (*divisioni*) to the margins and, following this model, the 1576 *edition princeps* published by Sermantelli does not print them. See Jelena Todorović, *Dante and the Dynamics of Textual Exchange* (New York: Fordham University Press, 2016), pp. 4–6.

19 In *The Body of Beatrice*, Harrison investigates in depth this generative power delegated to Beatrice.

called a *performative* utterance in J. L. Austin's sense of the term.[20] These kinds of words, in their precise arrangement, are re-performed as a real utterance by someone else and every time they establish a 'now' of the event. Jonathan Culler aptly distinguishes this kind of *performance* from Austin's *performativity* and specifically credits the lyric with it.[21] Yet there is something else: These words are not simply the presentation of a feeling, situation, or condition with which the reader can empathize or identify herself. Even for the reader, it is not a matter of external referentiality. In the lyric poem the repeatable *verbal gesture* is the real gesture. Language and act coincide in a performance that does not actualize anything but itself in the external world. The re-enactment or re-citation of such gestures, which always entails an interplay between memories and expectations, could have a role in the self-recognition of the literary genre across centuries. By re-citing these gestures, perhaps, one could even act as a lyric subject.

20 John L. Austin, *How to Do Things with Words* (Cambridge, MA: Harvard University Press, 1975).

21 Culler, *Theory of the Lyric*, pp. 125–31.

Recovery

CLIO NICASTRO

Despite the increasing incidence of eating disorders, very few films have addressed these conditions in particular and, what's more, most of the US-American mainstream fiction films seem to be built on anachronistic clichés hardly depicting the broad array of eating disorders. As a proof — however controversial and partial — of the dramatic and manifold presence of this health issue in our society, the latest, fifth edition of the Diagnostic and Statistical Manual of Mental Disorders (DSM-5),[1] in 2013, has reclassified and expanded the types of eating disorders [abbreviated in the following as 'ED'], acknowledging ones which are less visible, either because they do not conspicuously mark the body or because they fit socially accepted obsessions and practices — e.g., strict diets, orthorexia, and over-exercising.

I am particularly interested in looking at the cinematic misrepresentation of these conditions because it crucially

1 *Diagnostic and Statistical Manual of Mental Disorders, Fifth Edition*, DSM-5, ed. by American Psychiatric Association (Washington, DC: American Psychiatric Publishing, 2013).

sheds light on a discrepancy between the temporality of ED symptoms and the narrative of recovery. The latter often merely serves the purpose of framing the film's protagonists' dramatic development, namely the story of their ED experience, according to the traditional plot structure of beginning, middle, and end, which in most cases winds up in an implausible 'therapeutic happy end'. In this sense, 'to recover' meets the classic definition of 'returning to a normal state of health, mind, or strength', as if nothing happened 'in the meantime', and as if 'to heal' meant 'to forget'. Pointing out the entanglement between ED symptoms and the process of recovery itself is not a way to deny the condition, to push it back into a hidden and secret realm, where no one is around, but it is rather a proposition to find a different angle to read the 'externally' evident expressions of discomfort, especially when taking into account less easily detectable, less circumscribed nutritional disorders. Comparison of medical, psychological, and sociological explanatory models of eating disorders with one another shows that anorexia, bulimia, binge eating, and chronic dieting have not one single cause, but this is not the sense one gets from watching most films about ED. Not eating — overeating and binge eating mainly remain out of frame — is most often shown as a response to life stress or as corresponding to a desire to be more fashionable or more efficient. Even if statistics show that anorexia, in particular, afflicts mostly women, the focus on a single affected constituency not only marginalizes afflicted minorities, but also hinders understanding the complexity and multifaceted nature of the disorder, at the risk of reducing it to a contemporary form of hysteria.[2] In this connection, Abigail Bray illuminates how such a perspective fuels the risk

---

2 Cf. Greta Olson, *Reading Eating Disorders: Writings on Bulimia and*

gender and racial clichés. As Hadley Freeman has noticed, the 'unconventional' psychiatrist is a man, 'the nurse is a woman, Ellen's mother and her girlfriend are both self-obsessed, her father is absent but hard-working. The one male anorexia patient is wise and selfless in a way none of the female patients are, and he, along with the male doctor, helps to "save" Ellen.'[4]

Over the last years, journalists[5] and academics from the social sciences, cultural and gender studies[6] have been drawing attention to the way in which discriminatory assumptions are in play in and being validated by narrative representations of ED. But despite the longstanding debate about the negative influence of media on the proliferation of ED, there is very little research on the significance of the aesthetics employed in representing ED in narrative visual media.[7] And yet, when cinema meets such a

4 Hadley Freeman, 'To the Bone Confirms There Are (Almost) No Good Movies about Anorexia', *Guardian*, 12 July 2017 <https://www.theguardian.com/film/2017/jul/12/to-the-bone-confirms-there-are-almost-no-good-movies-about-anorexia> [accessed 21 September 2018].

5 See Elisabeth King, 'Are Movies about Eating Disorders Fundamentally Uncinematic?', *Pacific Standard*, 14 July 2017 <https://psmag.com/social-justice/how-to-make-a-movie-about-a-lonely-terrible-experience> [accessed 21 September 2018]; Michelle Konstantinovsky, 'Eating Disorders Do Not Discriminate: Puncturing the Dangerous Myth That Only White Women Get Eating Disorders', *Slate*, 20 March 2014 <http://www.slate.com/articles/double_x/doublex/2014/03/eating_disorders_and_women_of_color_anorexia_and_bulimia_are_not_just_white.html> [accessed 21 September 2018].

6 See Roxane Gay, *Hunger* (New York: HarperCollins, 2017); Gitte Marianne Hansen, *Femininity, Self-Harm and Eating Disorders in Japan. Navigating Contradiction in Narrative and Visual Culture* (London: Routledge, 2016); Helen Malson and Maree Burns, *Critical Feminist Approaches to Eating Dis/Orders* (London: Routledge, 2009).

7 See Su Holmes, '(Un)twisted: Talking Back to Media Representations of Eating Disorders', *Journal of Gender Studies*, 27.3 (May 2016), pp. 1–16.

sensitive and persistent social problem, different aesthetic practices can dramatically affect particular kinds of audiences — for instance those who suffer from ED themselves as distinct from those who want to learn more about it. Films are not, or not only, meant to reproduce conventional conceptions of reality but they can go beyond medical statistics, pathological categories, and predictable ways of instilling empathy. In 2016, the writer and artist Jessie Kahnweiler directed the webseries *The Skinny* to sensitize people to those eating disorders like bulimia that tend to be less commonly represented than anorexia, since, despite their exponential rise, they are less conspicuous, that is, cannot be recognized as easily on the patient's body. Kahnweiler, who herself has been suffering for many years from bulimia, points out how films about eating disorders are not at all realistic since they don't reveal the disgusting and shameful aspects of binging, purging, and throwing up. Her attempt to move the issue out of the clinical space and into daily life by showing eating disorders in their ordinary, mundane environment where they become invisible — yet very present in the daily schedule of the protagonist — is a remarkable alternative to unrealistic plots with compulsively happy endings. Nonetheless, visibility and eating disorders are much more entangled than Kahnweiler brings to light in her intentionally grotesque depiction of bulimia. If Kahnweiler's provocation draws attention to shame and secrecy by overexposing bulimia symptoms, it uncovers only some of the numerous elements at stake in analysing eating disorders through both an individual and socio-political lens.

The question of how ED should be represented suggests a more general question: how to account for mental disorders, especially when the disorders' borders blur into a chronic life background and their supposed symptoms approach what Lauren Berlant, within her theory of 'slow death', calls 'self-interruptive' gestures.[8] In a similar vein, perhaps, a more detailed and useful way of accounting for the pervasiveness of ED could be found outside of those places where recovery officially takes place (clinics, hospitals, therapists). By insisting on the interior settings of the clinic or the family, films that deal with ED tend, in fact, to adopt a psychological point of view without enlarging their frame to the dimensions of production and consumption that are so central in neoliberal societies. Eating disorders touch, in fact, both the private and the public spheres and by doing so, they reveal transformations, obsessions, and contradictions of society at large. The paradoxical way, for instance, in which eating disorders are stigmatized while at the same time 'low-fat', 'healthy' food and dieting have become one of the most profitable businesses. Not to mention the medicalization of political issues through the discourses of public shaming disguised by a rhetoric of 'individual responsibility' and the introjection of control. In this sense it is interesting to look at the obsession with the body not merely as a form of individual as well as collective narcissism. In the words of Micki Mcgee 'the desire to invent a life is no longer evidence of narcissistic self-involvement or an emancipatory countercultural impulse, but rather is increasingly required as a new form of 'immaterial labour' — mental, social and emotional tasks — required for participation in the labour market".[9] In this perspective, the desire to shape and con-

8 Lauren Berlant, 'Slow Death (Obesity, Sovereignty, Lateral Agency)', in *Cruel Optimism*, (Durham, NC: Duke University Press, 2011), pp. 95–119.

9 Micki McGee, *Self Help, Inc.: Makeover Culture in American Life* (Oxford: Oxford University Press, 2005), p. 24.

trol the body is yet another piece of the puzzle that in Silvia Federici's historical reconstruction of modernity from the seventeenth century onwards, sees body and capital as inextricably linked,[10] or to be precise, the female body and capital. Zooming out from the pathological frame in this sense is indeed not a way to relativize the severe medical consequence of eating disorders, but a way to read the macro- and micro-expressivity of their symptoms. A teleological narrative of recovery occludes a crucial aspect of the temporality of eating disorders, namely the experience of being condemned to a 'not yet', barred from recognizing one's self as part of a story in the name of a phantasmal true self still to be realized. It is perhaps in this sense that, once again, we should shift our gaze to the causes of the overwhelmingly gendered epidemic in the socio-historical roots of this phantasm.

10 Silvia Federici, *The Caliban and the Witch: Woman, the Body and Primitive Accumulation* (New York: Autonomedia, 2004).

Reenactment

Errant Images in Contemporary Art

CRISTINA BALDACCI

The following remarks are intended to serve as an introduction to *reenactment*, which was the topic of an international symposium I co-organized at the ICI Berlin in November 2017.[1]

By 'visual errancy' I mean the wandering of certain images — also intended as forms and gestures — over time, which contemporary artists appropriate from the archives *tout court*, but also from the archive understood in a broader sense, as a heterotopic space where all cultural images potentially converge and remain in a state of

1 The symposium 'Over and Over and Over Again: Re-enactment Strategies in Contemporary Arts and Theory' <https://www.ici-berlin.org/events/over-and-over> [accessed 18 December 2018], organized together with Clio Nicastro and Arianna Sforzini, aimed at following and retracing the notion of reenactment along three parallel approaches: the archive, the arts, and curatorial practice. The proceedings of the conference will be published in the same book series as the current volume, 'Cultural Inquiry'.

flux. This appropriation is then followed by a reactivation, which usually also undergoes a process of manipulation and/or migration from one medium to another, and by recirculation that gives the images new values, meanings, and configurations.[2]

As special creators of images, willingly or not, artists have to deal with a collective visual tradition that relates to a timeless or at least multi-layered and anachronic time. They have in fact always been engaged with what came before; with the gesture of a more or less conscious appropriation, with the repetition, as a synonym for reinterpretation and renewal, of a visual heritage made of 'originals',[3] whose attribution or provenance is mostly not declared (and not necessarily relevant). No matter how they have been called throughout the twentieth century, based on their different connotations and contexts — be it archetypes (Jung), *Pathosformeln* (Warburg), or reproductions (Benjamin) — in the end they are all recurrent images that emerge again and travel across time.[4]

It is hardly news that art does not come out of a void,

---

2 See *Dear Aby Warburg, What Can Be Done with Images?*, ed. by Ines Rütinger and Eva Schmidt (Heidelberg: Kehrer, 2012); and *Les Artistes iconographes/Artists as Iconographers*, ed. by Garance Chabert and Aurélien Mole (Paris: Empire Books-Villa du Parc, 2018).

3 On this topic see, among others, Sylviane Agacinski, 'Anachronisms of Art: Style and Medium', in *Time Passing: Modernity and Nostalgia*, trans. by Jody Gladding (New York: Columbia University Press, 2003), pp. 105–36, especially p. 111; and 'Images of Images: The Survival and Repetition of Forms. A Conversation between Massimiliano Gioni and Andrea Pinotti', in *To Write an Image*, ed. by Vincenzo de Bellis (Milan: Mousse Publishing, 2015), pp. 17–27.

4 The image's wandering has to be understood not only as an external motion but also, as Giorgio Agamben suggests, as an internal one, since 'every image is animated by an antinomous polarity' that breaks the myth of its fixity. See Giorgio Agamben, 'Notes on Gesture', in *Infancy and History: The Destruction of Experience*, trans. by Liz Heron (London: Verso, 1993), pp. 133–40 (p. 139).

since it has always been produced in reference to already existing images, mixing different temporalities and codes. As Jay Bolter and Richard Grusin highlight in their book on remediation — by quoting Stanley Cavell's study on the ontology of cinema (*The World Viewed*, 1979) —, despite the obsession historians and critics have had for novelty, the task of the (modern) artist has always been 'one of creating not a new instance of his art, but a new medium in it'. That implies, of course, that the 'novelty' resembles a reinvention or rearrangement of what already exists more than a total revolution.[5]

And here we come to reenactment, a term that I would like to introduce as a possible substitute for 'remake', which for me also has a closer affinity with the meaning Bolter and Grusin attribute to remediation as the act of 'refashioning'; especially — but not only — when dealing with (digital) images and time-based art, that is, film, video, and performance.

Where does the word reenactment, so often used today, come from? And how did it happen that, from historical discourse[6] and the relationship with the archive and with time,[7] it has now entered both the artistic and the curatorial practice?

---

5 Cf. Jay D. Bolter and Richard A. Grusin, *Remediation: Understanding New Media* (Cambridge, MA: MIT Press, 1999), p. 270.

6 Cf. especially Robin G. Collingwood, *The Idea of History* (Oxford: Clarendon Press, 1946); William H. Dray, *History as Re-enactment: R. G. Collingwood's Idea of History* (Oxford: Oxford University Press, 1995); and Vanessa Agnew, 'History's Affective Turn: Historical Reenactment and Its Work in the Present', *Rethinking History*, 11.3 (2007), pp. 299–312.

7 From this perspective, as Wolfgang Ernst argues in his writings, it seems that even digital technologies have accustomed us to a continuous reenactment. See Wolfgang Ernst, *The Delayed Present: Media-Induced Tempor(e)alities & Techno-Traumatic Irritations of 'the Contemporary'* (Berlin: Sternberg Press, 2017), pp. 9–10.

As a verb and derivative of the Middle English 'enacten', it has been used since the seventeenth century. Over time, 'to re-enact' has taken on different connotations depending on the specific context of its use. To name two of the most relevant: it can mean 'to repeat the actions (of an earlier event or incident)' as well as 'to act or perform again'.[8] The first definition is less interesting for my argument because it mainly relates to the trend of 'Living History', that is, to historical revival as a form of entertainment and collective memory constructed through the act of 'making experience'.[9] The second definition is related to the former one but goes directly to the heart of the matter. It does indeed relate to the performing arts, where the noun reenactment originated — yet within a wider perspective and an increasing persistence from the 1990s onwards —, connecting it to other artistic idioms. Although in both cases it constitutes an attempt to bring history back to life (or to the present), unlike the act of restaging related to 'Living History', which implies the idea of replicating as faithfully as possible the original event, reenactment as an art form is an interpretative gesture that never produces a true repetition. As is well known, it was Antonin Artaud who once said that a gesture in theatre can 'never be made the same way twice'.[10]

---

8 'Reenact', *Merriam-Webster Online Dictionary* <https://www.merriam-webster.com/dictionary/reenact> [accessed 18 December 2018].

9 See, for instance, Marvin Carlson, 'Living History, Re-enactment', in *Performance Studies: Key Words, Concepts and Theories*, ed. by Bryan Reynolds (London: Palgrave, 2014), pp. 84–90.

10 Artaud quoted in Amelia Jones, 'The Now and the Has Been: Paradoxes of Live Art in History', in *Perform, Repeat, Record: Live Art in History*, ed. by Amelia Jones and Adrian Heathfield (Bristol: Intellect, 2012), p. 11.

One of the most interesting aspects of reenactment as reappropriation and reembodiment is the role of the artist's body as a medium that gives form and substance, not only to actions by other performers — as it happened in *Seven Easy Pieces*, the most celebrated as well as criticized work that Marina Abramović staged at the Guggenheim Museum in New York in 2005 —,[11] but also to artworks that come from different eras, contexts, and languages.[12]

By staging and embodying anew existing images that the artist-performer can, from time to time, take either from his/her own repertoire and the repertoire of others, or from art history and the visual imaginary, cultural traditions are reactivated and travel over time in the form of ritualized behaviours or even scores — where score, taken from the musical domain, is to be understood in a broader sense as code, namely a system of signs.[13] In this way, the body becomes similar to an 'atlas of gestures',[14]

11 *Seven Easy Pieces* included reenactments of two of Abramović's previous performances as well as five actions by Vito Acconci, Joseph Beuys, VALIE EXPORT, Bruce Nauman, and Gina Pane. Cf. Amelia Jones, '"The Artist Is Present": Artistic Re-enactments and the Impossibility of Presence', *TDR: The Drama Review*, 55.1 (2011), pp. 16–45, especially p. 18.

12 Seen from Hans Belting's anthropological perspective, the body is here at the same time the locus and the medium (through which it becomes picture) of the image. Cf. Hans Belting, *An Anthropology of Images: Picture, Medium, Body*, trans. by Thomas Dunlap (Princeton: Princeton University Press, 2011).

13 Cf., among others, Diana Taylor, *The Archive and the Repertoire: Performing Cultural Memory in the Americas* (Durham, NC: Duke University Press, 2003); André Lepecki, 'The Body as Archive: Will to Re-enact and the Afterlives of Dances', *Dance Research Journal*, 42.2 (2010), pp. 28–48; and *Recréer/Scripter. Mémoires et transmissions des œuvres performatives et chorégraphiques contemporaines*, ed. by Anne Bénichou (Dijon: Presses du réel, 2015).

14 See, to name but a few, Virgilio Sieni's choreographies, from which this expression comes, Tino Sehgal's 'constructed situations', and Alexandra Pirici's and Manuel Pelmuş' *Immaterial Retrospective* (2013) and *Public Collection* (2015).

that is, an archive of movements, experiences, and forms with a strong symbolic charge; a place for the *Nachleben* (survival) that challenges the traditional idea of heritage and at the same time renews the modalities of conservation, presentation/representation, and of the circulation of knowledge.

This is the case, for instance, in Alexandra Pirici's choreographed 'ongoing actions', where the performers' bodies become media that translate and transmit cultural memory and visual history as living images or counter-narratives. The artist started being noticed in the art scene in 2011, when a group of performers embodied specific historical monuments in public spaces to highlight issues of memory and politics, partly echoing Joseph Beuys' 'social sculpture'.[15] Her breakthrough happened when she participated, together with Manuel Pelmuş, in the 55th Venice Biennale (2013) presenting *An Immaterial Retrospective of the Venice Biennale* in the Romanian pavilion. On that occasion, Pirici and Pelmuş demonstrated that history, and especially the history of art, can be recollected by transforming the actual object-document (here a selection of artworks made with different media and shown at the Biennale since its foundation in 1895) into an action, as an immaterial testimony. The fact that a work of art, usually fetishized as a monument or commodity, can be turned into an image-gesture, thus freed from any specific substance and stable shape, becomes here a guarantee for its afterlife. Currently, Pirici's actions (e.g., *Delicate Instruments of Engagement*, 2017) have come to criticize canonical fixations, data sovereignty, and filter mechanisms

15 Another important point of reference for Pirici is the French choreographer Jérôme Bel, who is known for his 'non-dance'.

within the digital realm by remixing a repertoire of images, situations, and even Internet memes.

Apart from the body, the rehabilitation of images and histories — especially the ones that have been forgotten, never written, censored or are largely lacking testimonies — occurs through the reconstruction of artworks and exhibitions, and especially through the questioning and setting in motion of the archive. In the specific case of exhibitions and artworks, the more they are left incomplete, transient, or 'immaterial', the more their reenactment is effective, both because it leaves room for a freer translation/interpretation, and because, in an unfinished or unfinishable object, there is always something unexplored to be brought to light.[16]

Furthermore, when archives are interrogated in a work of research and reconstruction, the recovery of the past and reenactment of already existing images take place through a montage/display of heterogeneous materials. This process is comparable to a 'dramaturgy of information', an expression John Rajchman has used for the historical revaluation that occurs through a particular kind of philosophical exhibition, his main example being Jean-François Lyotard's *Les Immatériaux* (Centre Pompidou, Paris, 1985), where the task of expressing ideas is entrusted exclusively to images;[17] or better, to 'chains of images',

16 See John Rajchman, '*Les Immatériaux* or How to Construct the History of Exhibitions', *Tate Papers*, 12 (2009) <https://www.tate.org.uk/research/publications/tate-papers/12/les-immateriaux-or-how-to-construct-the-history-of-exhibitions> [accessed 18 December 2018]; and Cristina Baldacci and Clio Nicastro, 'Il Bilderatlas Mnemosyne ri-visitato: una mostra e un convegno a Karlsruhe', *La rivista di Engramma*, 142 (2017) <http://www.engramma.it/eOS/index.php?id_articolo=3086> [accessed 18 December 2018].

17 Rajchman, '*Les Immatériaux*', n. p.

that is, dynamic and operative structures, similar to constellations or clusters, which presuppose a set of interdependent narrative instances (pre-production, production, post-production).[18]

When artists instead deal with images that re-emerge 'mute' from either the archive or an indefinite time and context, one of their first concerns is usually to understand how those images can be effectively reactivated and resignified without betraying them. In most cases, the reenactment of mainly archival materials is a unique opportunity to put history in motion through original counter-narratives.[19] History, then, is transformed from a succession of supposedly universally significant facts, which usually produce and reiterate a dominant cultural narrative, into a counter-history where archival documents are revived or, if necessary, recreated *ex novo* (through fiction) as witnesses and personal devices of memory and resistance. At the heart of this, there is the desire to initiate a rewriting and deinstitutionalizing or decolonizing process that starts right from the images, and that presents, more than a remembering technique, a 'working through' [*Durcharbeitung*], as Lyotard wrote quoting Freud.[20]

---

18 Philippe Parreno's exhibitions, which cannot be examined here, are emblematic of this attitude. Cf. *Philippe Parreno: H{n)ypn(y}osis/Hypothesis*, ed. by Andrea Lissoni (Milan: Mousse Publishing, 2017).

19 See, in particular, Sven Lütticken, *History in Motion: Time in the Age of the Moving Image* (Berlin: Sternberg Press, 2013); and Cristina Baldacci, 'Re-enactment e altre storie. Dall'archivio alla contro-narrazione per immagini nell'arte contemporanea', *La rivista di Engramma*, 150 (2017), pp. 41–48 <http://www.engramma.it/eOS/index.php?id_articolo=3215> [accessed 18 December 2018].

20 Cf. Jean-François Lyotard, *The Inhuman: Reflections on Time*, trans. by Rachel Bowlby and Geoffrey Bennington (Cambridge: Polity, 1991), p. 26.

This additional narrative guides the viewer when looking at images and is also a way of reflecting on two central aspects of the archival and historical reenactment: Firstly, who accesses the archive, and, in particular, who 'recovers' archival images? Secondly, how can artists make those images accessible again, overcoming the tricky questions of authoriality, property, and legitimacy of the (photographic) image as a document that, in theory, should present reality instead of representing it through different modes of interpretation?[21] This is particularly evident in the case of time-based art that 'continuously remodels and modulates history — for instance by actualizing the historical record in the form of images that in turn help to shape the on-going production of new history in today's temporal economy'.[22]

Alongside the restaging of performances by artists, actors, and dancers as homage to or dialogue with their precursors, in recent years another form of reenactment has been emerging as a decisive procedure of contemporary art at large: the reconstruction of works and exhibitions of the twentieth century.[23] This tendency can be interpreted as a consequence of postconceptual art and — in Peter Osborne's words — its 'process of ontological homogenization', for which 'the artistic materiality of the work

21 For Allan Sekula, 'the archive constitutes the paradigm or iconic system from which photographic "statements" are constructed.' Cf. Allan Sekula, 'Reading an Archive: Photography Between Labour and Capital', in *The Photography Reader*, ed. by Liz Wells (London: Routledge, 2003), pp. 443–52 (p. 445).

22 Lütticken, *History in Motion*, p. 26.

23 The endeavour undertaken by the Fondazione Prada in Venice with the reenactment of the legendary *When Attitudes Become Form* (1969) in 2013 is one of the main examples — even if not the first — of this trend and has set its standard. See *When Attitudes Become Form: Bern 1969/Venice 2013*, ed. by Germano Celant (Milan: Fondazione Prada, 2013).

and its documentary function are combined', as well as 'a growing indifference between the artwork and its documentation, at the level of the collection' and therefore of archival and curatorial practices.[24] But it also reveals the desire to restore concreteness to what is impermanent or has survived only as a ghost-image, on one side, and to give a place in art history to those events that have remained outside the predominant cultural tradition, on the other. The absence or incompleteness of the preexisting artefact hence becomes a prophecy and a condition of its rebirth.

That's why this meta-reflexive and historiographic approach, which stems also from the fear of elusiveness and loss of thingliness and sometimes takes on tautological aspects, must not be mistaken for an academic or reactionary exercise — an association Boris Groys has made in relation to art documentation and specifically to installation.[25] It should rather be considered as an invitation to look further and envisage a multifaceted art history that moves away from the restrictively Western gaze and from conventional categories, opening up to transculturation.

Inside the museum and other art spaces, reenacting specific exhibitions and artworks is a way to create history through a direct comparison of the 're-habilitated' object-image with the present to offer a possible understanding of the past that gives preference to a visual and performative, sometimes immersive, approach.[26]

---

24 See Peter Osborne, 'Archive as Afterlife and Life of Art', in *WERE IT AS IF: Beyond an Institution that Is*, ed. by Bik van der Pol and Defne Ayas (Rotterdam: Witte de With Center for Contemporary Art, 2017), pp. 49–53 (p. 52).

25 See Boris Groys, 'Art in the Age of Biopolitics: From Artwork to Art Documentation', in *Art Power* (Cambridge, MA: MIT Press, 2008), pp. 53–65.

26 This attitude often goes together with two different practices: first, the search for original documentation and its gathering in archives newly

There remains, of course, a latent risk in this practice: any repeatability can easily result in a seriality that produces empty simulacra and multiples. Thus, far from presenting a guarantee of continuity in time,[27] reenactment can degenerate into a market strategy of fetishization that merely seeks to satisfy the collectors' desire for possession.

---

constituted; second, the publication of voluminous catalogues or entire series dedicated to the study of one single artwork or exhibition. See for instance the book series 'One Work' and 'Exhibition Histories' published by Afterall Books.

27 Cf. *Serial/Portable Classic: The Greek Canon and its Mutations*, ed. by Salvatore Settis (Milan: Fondazione Prada, 2015).

Rehabilitation I

BIRKAN TAŞ

Rehabilitation. (*Noun*). The action of restoring someone to health or normal life through training and therapy after imprisonment, addiction, or illness.

oxforddictionaries.com

In *The History of Disability*, Henri-Jacques Stiker reflects on the exclusion of people with disabilities in western discourse and the emergence of the modern concept of rehabilitation in the twentieth century, and writes:

> The concepts of 're-' [...] come at logical intervals: to reintegrate, we must redeploy; to redeploy, we must retrain; to retrain, we must rehabilitate (the body and its organs, intellect and movement). But there is another way of sequencing all this: we can replace what is missing, and this leads to retraining, and that to redeploying then to reintegrating, and that is rehabilitation. Along this axis of specific action, rehabilitation always comes at the end, as the most specific action or as the most generic.

> Rehabilitation is co-extensive with disabilities and their extension in time.[1]

Disabilities and their extension in time structure rehabilitative practices that, on the most generic or specific level, conceive of disability in a framework of loss and lack, which needs to be compensated. Bringing back a former capacity involves individual effort in the present, which shapes the course of the future in a prognostic manner. In this developmentalist framework, rehabilitation operates according to a medical view that sees impairment as a deviation from the norm, a biological deficiency to be eliminated in order to achieve increased independence, and an improved quality of life. Stiker's historical analysis shows that western cultural responses to disability regard the body as perennially incomplete and disability as a temporary obstacle. Within this matrix, 'if you devote sufficient resources, it is possible to reduce the distance and bring each person, however great the burden she carries, to reoccupy a normal place in the group of the able (normal)'.[2] The distance that needs to be reduced though rehabilitation is embedded in a temporality in which disabilities are considered to be aberrant and anachronistic because they do not fit into the 'machinery of production, [and] consumption'.[3]

In France and Britain, modern practices of rehabilitation emerged in the aftermath of World War I, when hundreds of thousands of injured soldiers returned home. Following the juridical discourse on work-related accidents codified in the last decades of the nineteenth century, during the post-war years, 'replacement for a deficit' became a

1 Henri-Jacques Stiker, *The History of Disability* (Ann Arbor: University of Michigan Press, 1999), p. 128.

2 Ibid., p. 135.

3 Ibid., p. 128.

generalized objective of modern notions of rehabilitation, and extended to people with disabilities.[4] Stiker reads this paradigm of deficiency and loss in relation to a desire to 're-cover and reenter the competition of the industrial world and technological society'.[5] He mentions that during this period, in France and Britain, the word 'handicap' replaced other words with negative prefixes such as 'infirm', 'invalid', 'impotent', and 'incapable' previously used to define people with mental and physical disabilities. In the eighteenth century, handicap meant the extra weight imposed upon a superior horse or the disadvantage imposed on a competitor in favor of an inferior one. It thus emerged as a negative value in a context of rivalry where some bodies had to catch up with others. Such shifts in language imply parallels between France and Britain in their cultural responses to disability. The modern concept of rehabilitation emerges at the same time with this lexical change, which, in Julie Passanante Elman's words, is entangled with 'healthy bodies and healthy economies, once threatened and then restored'.[6]

Stiker's historical analysis explores rehabilitation practices as forms of governmentality that are linked to economic profit. As a two-part process of identity and integration, emerging rehabilitation practices, primarily in France and Western Europe, aimed to relocate bodily and mental differences into the 'machinery of production, consumption', and work by standardizing human beings, and assimilating them into a unified social order.[7] For Stiker, 'the

4 Ibid., pp. 124–25.

5 Ibid., p. 150.

6 Julie Passanante Elman, *Chronic Youth: Disability, Sexuality, and U.S. Media Cultures of Rehabilitation* (New York: New York University Press, 2014), p. 14.

7 Stiker, *The History of Disability*, pp. 112–28.

demand to be like the others', which is implemented on juridical, administrative, and institutional levels, is based on oblivion, disappearance, conformity, and normalization.[8] Whereas in earlier eras disability stood for radical alterity, in the twentieth century western culture it came to mean a difference of degree on which rehabilitation came to operate as a social act of identification that would cause people with disabilities to disappear.[9] People with bodily differences, writes Stiker, 'are *established as a category to be reintegrated and thus to be rehabilitated.* Paradoxically, they are designated in order to be made to disappear, they are spoken of in order to be silenced.'[10] To put it differently, western modern conceptions of rehabilitation negate disability through their focus on adjustment and integration, whose success depends on the physical and social obliteration of disabilities.

The normative pull of rehabilitation both requires compliance and aims to make noncompliance with, let alone resistance to, societal norms unthinkable. As Robert McRuer writes, rehabilitation demands obedience: 'What we might call the rehabilitative contract [...] essentially stipulates that, in return for integration, no complaints will be made, no suggestions for how the world, and not the disabled body and mind, might be molded differently'.[11] For Elman, in this process of enforced assimilation to able-bodied normalcy, rehabilitation becomes coterminous with citizenship. She uses the term 'rehabilitative citizenship' to explain how seemingly apolitical notions of health or growth that shape rehabilitative practices are

8 Ibid., p. 133.

9 Ibid., p. 128.

10 Ibid., p. 134 [emphasis in the original].

11 Robert McRuer, *Crip Theory: Cultural Signs of Queerness and Disability* (New York: New York University Press, 2006), pp. 112–13.

deeply attached to 'what it means to be a good citizen'.[12] As an affective tool of self-governance, hegemonic forms of rehabilitation imply compulsory adaptation to societal inequalities.

While rehabilitation disguises itself as an apolitical and universal objective, crip theory and practices posit rehabilitation as historically contingent, political, and embedded in the cultural history of dominant economic forces, which attach norms, values, and meaning to what bodies should do or be.[13] Crip theory and practices also criticize the rigidity of 'narratives of progress' that shape rehabilitative practices in western culture, which obscure the continuities between the past and the present, and the ways in which the past endures in the present in different ways, as Heather Love discusses in relation to the politics of queer history.[14]

Robert McRuer and Merri Lisa Johnson situates this crip resistance to a homogenizing ideology within an epistemology, which they call 'cripistemology',[15] in an effort to rethink how we know what we know about disability 'as though it could be a thoroughly comprehended ob-

12 Elman, *Chronic Youth*, p. 16.

13 The word 'crip' comes from 'cripple', which has been and is used to describe pejoratively people with physical disabilities. It emerged in disability activism as an oppositional political response to ableism and to describe people with various disabilities and allies of disability culture and community. Like the term 'queer', which has taken on new meanings and political agendas within (and beyond) LGBT communities, crip theory and practices also gain political and analytical power beyond disability studies. Rather than aiming to fit into society as it is, crip theory, like queer theory, aims to transform society and probe the boundaries for imagining alternative futures and communities.

14 Heather Love, *Feeling Backward: Loss and the Politics of Queer History* (Cambridge, MA: Harvard University Press, 2007).

15 Merri Lisa Johnson and Robert McRuer, 'Cripistemologies: Introduction', *Journal of Literary & Cultural Disability Studies*, 8.2 (2014), pp. 127–47 (p. 128).

ject of knowledge'.[16] Cripistemology questions dominant claims of knowledge production, 'destabilizes the category of disability and opens its borders to include more and different kinds of bodily and affective experiences'.[17] It puts notions of ability and disability into a crisis, not to resolve them once and for all, but to attend to the question which bodies/minds/impairments are naturalized, made invisible, or publicly excluded. Cripistemology is about, in Arun Saldanha's words, 'letting yourself be destabilized by the radical alterity of the other, in seeing his or her difference not as a threat but as a resource to question your own position in the world'.[18] This is part of a political and relational process, which requires the ability to affect and be affected by the shifting abilities of different bodies as part of a critical category of cultural and historical analysis.

For me, an important part of such a politics of noncompliance that aims to *crip* hegemonic rehabilitative practices entails embracing vulnerability as a condition of becoming, and attending to ways in which certain populations or bodies are made more vulnerable to inequalities. Subsumed under a linear and developmentalist neoliberal temporal logic, the conventional framing of vulnerability as an obstacle to be eliminated for maximum efficiency and autonomy needs to be challenged. As Judith Butler argues, we must pay attention to the 'mass difference of conditions that distribute vulnerability across the globe'.[19] For her, the ethical task lies in accepting responsibility

16 Ibid., p. 130.

17 Ibid., p. 135.

18 Quoted in Jasbir Puar, 'Prognosis Time: Towards a Geopolitics of Affect, Debility and Capacity', *Women & Performance: A Journal of Feminist Theory*, 19.2 (2009), pp. 161–72 (p. 169).

19 Judith Butler, *Precarious Life: The Powers of Mourning and Violence* (London: Verso, 2004), p. 31.

for its differential allocation, albeit in many affective, economic, social, cultural, legal, and political contexts.[20] It's the task of politics, as Butler sees it, to challenge the ways in which vulnerability is differentially allocated across bodies as mechanisms of control or oppression. In other words, it is not only about identifying which populations *are* vulnerable but also about focusing on situations that *make* certain people vulnerable.

Drawing on how certain vulnerabilities and disabilities are institutionally, economically, and culturally praised or devalued is crucial to challenge paternalistic rehabilitative norms. To put it differently, politicizing or *cripping* vulnerability and interdependence and their value in human lives can help us resist the individualizing and assimilationist ideologies that compulsory rehabilitation perpetuate in their claim to increased independence and similarity. The uncertainty of vulnerability that shapes our interaction with the world encompasses a certain politics of rehabilitation, not just as an individual affair, but as a social one. As a source of hope and connection, politicizing vulnerability involves a critique of rehabilitative practices that pin their hopes solely on the future elimination of vulnerability, and looks at the ways in which invulnerability as mastery is selectively allocated to certain bodies in the past and present.

The negative connotations of vulnerability that link it solely with deficit or loss of autonomy create paternalistic rehabilitative responses or idealized care relations. Thus, challenging univocal definitions of vulnerability is an ethical task insofar as vulnerability is constitutive of life. For me, an openness to vulnerability is embedded in a politics of hope insofar as to hope opens one up to disappointment,

---

20 Judith Butler, *Frames of War: When is Life Grievable?* (London: Verso, 2009), p. 3.

pain, injury, and despair. It emphasizes an openness to risk. One may work to minimize the risks involved, yet it is impossible to completely eliminate them. This is not a form of hope, therefore, that envisions a future where vulnerabilities, disabilities, or impairments are eliminated for good. It is a form of hope that challenges what counts as a normal life or a normal body and embraces bodily differences and human diversity as constitutive of life.

Rehabilitation II

BIRKAN TAŞ

Lorenza Böttner was a Chilean-German trans woman and performance artist, born in 1959 in Chile. When she was eight years old, both of her arms were amputated after a severe accident in which she was electrocuted and fell from an electrical tower. At the age of fourteen, two months after the Chilean *coup d'etat,* she went to West Germany for plastic surgery and moved to Lichtenau. She studied painting at the Kassel School of Art and submitted a thesis entitled 'Behindert?', which explored the category of disability and the history of mouth and foot painters.[1] She

1 Paul B. Preciado, 'Lives and Works of Lorenza Böttner', *South as a State of Mind,* 9 [documenta 14 #4] ([2017]) <https://www.documenta14.de/en/south/25298_lives_and_works_of_lorenza_boettner> [accessed 10 December 2018]. Preciado served as curator of public programming for the documenta 14. He is also the curator of 'Lorenza Böttner. Requiem for the Norm', the most comprehensive retrospective of Böttner's work to date, co-produced by the La Virreina Centre de la Imatge, Barcelona and Württembergischer Kunstverein Stuttgart <http://ajuntament.barcelona.cat/lavirreina/en/exhibitions/requiem-norm/236> and <https://www.wkv-stuttgart.de/en/program/2019/exhibitions/lorenza-boettner-requiem-for-the-norm/> [accessed 13 January 2019].

presented many public performances combining dance and painting in Munich, San Francisco, New York, and New Mexico.[2]

Lorenza moved to Germany for rehabilitation, but refused to use prosthetic arms and learned to paint with her feet and mouth. If, in Julie Passanante Elman's words, 'rehabilitation, at its core, is a self-making project involving perpetual self-discipline and self-surveillance', Lorenza's bodily and artistic performances *crip* rehabilitation by refusing to return to the racetrack of ability, masculinity, and compulsory heterosexuality that modern normalizing rehabilitative practices reserved for her.[3] As Paul Preciado writes about her for the documenta14, which included several of her drawings, paintings, and video work: 'if medical discourse and modes of representation aim to desexualize and degender the impaired body, Lorenza's performance work eroticized the trans-armless body, endowing it with sexual and political potency'.[4]

Modern conceptions of rehabilitation regard disability as a temporary obstacle that needs to be readjusted in order to approximate normalcy embedded in an economy of autonomy and independence. In this temporal economy of 'rehabilitative citizenship', bodily differences are to be eliminated through the approximation of a supposed normalcy for maximum control and efficiency.[5] Lorenza's rejection of prosthetic arms and conventional gender roles

---

2 Carl Fischer, *Queering the Chilean Way: Cultures of Exceptionalism and Sexual Dissidence, 1965–2015* (New York: Palgrave Macmillan, 2016), pp. 205–09.

3 Julie Passanante Elman, *Chronic Youth: Disability, Sexuality, and U.S. Media Cultures of Rehabilitation* (New York: New York University Press, 2014), p. 14.

4 Preciado, 'Lives and Works of Lorenza Böttner'.

5 Elman, *Chronic Youth*, p. 16.

make her body permanently anachronistic inasmuch as reintegration to modern society requires upholding and sustaining the able-bodied (and heteronormative) norms embedded in a developmentalist 'chrononormative timing of bodies'.[6] A comment under the video *Lorenza* (1991) posted on *Vimeo* illuminates this point: The commentator says, 'beautifully shot!' and then asks: 'Don't they use prosthetic devices these days?'[7] Apart from the ambiguity and objectifying tone of 'they', the comment reflects a cultural grammar of rehabilitation based on compliance and assimilation. The question operates within the temporal imaginary of compulsory rehabilitation, promoting prosthetic devices as a matter of technology and time, but not choice. If prosthetics were available to her by then, she must have used them. However, we learn from director Michael Stahlberg's reply to that comment that Lorenza did not like prosthetic devices, which he says 'were to [sic] cumbersome for him [sic]'.[8]

Having emerged in eighteenth-century English medical texts, prosthetics conventionally were meant to 'replace' missing limbs. According to David Serlin, following the Second World War, prosthetics operated within 'the fiercely heterosexual culture of rehabilitation medicine, especially its orthodox zeal to preserve the masculine status of disabled veterans'.[9] Thus, prosthetics emerged 'to re-

6 Elizabeth Freeman, *Time Binds: Queer Temporalities, Queer Histories* (Durham, NC: Duke University Press, 2010), p. 44.

7 *Lorenza: Portrait of an Artist*, dir. by Michael Stahlberg (Hochschule für Fernsehen und Film München, 1991) <https://vimeo.com/29793957> [accessed 10 December 2018].

8 Ibid.

9 Quoted in Margrit Shildrick, 'Border Crossings: The Technology of Disability and Desire', in *Culture, Theory, Disability: Encounters Between Disability Studies and Cultural Studies*, ed. by Anne Waldschmidt,

normalize the disabled [heterosexual] male body'.[10] Margrit Schildrick notes that the success of prosthetics 'was often measured in professional literature by the extent to which they enabled the wearer to engage in normal gender activities'.[11] In other words, approximating an image of a non-disabled body through rehabilitation and prosthetics is historically couched in an approximation and reclaiming of heterosexuality. By refusing to use prosthetics, Lorenza exposes 'the inherent plasticity of the body, and its multiple possibilities of transcorporeality' and refuses to follow a 'normative corporeality'.[12] Her unwillingness to use prosthetics, along with her gender nonconformity, problematizes normative assumptions about what a body can do, which bodies are regarded as whole and complete. She does not 'miss' anything and hence does not need any replacements.

In the video, Lorenza *crips* paternalistic rehabilitative responses to bodily injuries, responses that envision these injuries merely in terms of a lack to overcome or a deficiency to suppress. She rejects the demand to be like others. Rather than making her disability disappear by complying with modern prosthetic technologies, she shows how disability is integral to (her) art. When she talks about statues (e.g. Venus de Milo) that have no arms or legs due to injury, she insists that they 'have lost nothing of their beauty or aesthetic appeal'. As a foundational element of modern art, and an aesthetic value in itself, disability is a critical resource for thinking about human variation and difference, as disability scholar Tobin Siebers argues as

---

Hanjo Berressem, and Moritz Ingwersen (Bielefeld: Transcript, 2017), pp. 137–51 (p. 139).

10 Ibid., p. 139.

11 Ibid.

12 Ibid., pp. 138–40.

well. He defines aesthetics in relation to the sensations that some bodies feel in the presence of other bodies. That is to say, aesthetics is first and foremost an embodied affective encounter between bodies. What he names 'disability aesthetics' acts as a critical concept to show the presence of disability in modern aesthetics and also an aesthetic value in itself for future concerns. For Siebers, in most cases, it is the presence of disability that makes an artwork more beautiful and endure over time. He asks,

> [s]ince aesthetic feelings of pleasure and disgust are difficult to separate from political feelings of acceptance and rejection, what do objects representing disability tell us about the ideals of political community underlying works of art?[13]

In considering this question, one of the aesthetic values I find in Lorenza's work is the way it broadens our understanding of conventional modes of beauty. In her art, disability acts as a generative force. Lorenza does not want to be silenced. Nor does she want her disability to disappear. In her account, disability emerges as something that can be and is complete, whole, and desirable. Her artistic performances emphasize human variation, different abilities of bodies, and their right to non-compliance. The themes Lorenza chose in her paintings, such as police brutality and nudity, politicize the aesthetics of mouth and foot painting as well. Integrating disability as a critical category of analysis and aesthetic value, Lorenza's public performances and paintings treat disability as a unique source of creation in modern art. They subvert not only hegemonic cultural discourses surrounding images of disability that

13 Tobin Siebers, *Disability Aesthetics* (Ann Arbor: University of Michigan Press, 2010), p. 2.

discuss it in terms of tragedy, loss, tears, and frustration but also the stereotypical images of all disabled people wanting to be normal, cured, or rehabilitated. The dominant emphasis on cure and rehabilitation locates disability in bodies that need to be fixed, and hence controls and limits human variation and difference. For that reason, reflecting on the intricacies of disability and rehabilitation opens a space–time where new relations between bodies, objects, and environments as well as possible strategies for resistance against bodily norms can emerge.

Renewal

CLIO NICASTRO

The *Renewal of Pagan Antiquity* (*La rinascita del paganesimo antico*) is the title the art historian and librarian Gertrud Bing, together with Emma Cantimori, chose for the first collection of Aby Warburg's writings, released in 1966 in Florence by the publishing house La Nuova Italia.[1] The Italian volume was published more than a decade before the German original because Bing, who had been one of Warburg's closest collaborators, wanted to make up for Ernst Gombrich's failed attempt to sort out and select Warburg's texts. After the Warburgian library was relocated from Hamburg to London in order to preserve its material from the upcoming World War II,[2] its new director Gom-

1 Aby Warburg, *La rinascita del paganesimo antico. Contributi alla storia della cultura* (Florence: La Nuova Italia, 1996); in English as Aby Warburg, *The Renewal of Pagan Antiquity: Contributions to the Cultural History of the European Renaissance* (Los Angeles: Getty Center for the History of Art and the Humanities, 1999).

2 See Dorothea McEwan, 'A Tale of One Institute and Two Cities: The Warburg Institute', *Yearbook of the Research Centre for German and Austrian Exile Studies*, 1 (1999): *German-Speaking Exiles in Great Britain*, ed. by Ian Wallace, pp. 25–42.

brich — who later would write the first biography of Warburg[3] — was tasked with carrying on and concluding the publication of the Hamburg scholar's *Nachlass.* Each small historical and biographical detail is relevant to get a sense of the rich and assorted collection of images and words that Warburg put together in the intense period between the end of the nineteenth century and the beginning of the twentieth century. For those who, like Gombrich, did not take part in the *Warburg circle's* collective research,[4] it was surely harder to access both Warburg's fragmentary essayistic production, diaries, and notes, and the pictures from the legendary, albeit unfinished project *Atlas Mnemosyne,* whose tables had been collected, assembled, and displayed in various formats for several decades.[5] The attempt to reconstruct the *Atlas* is, indeed, a never-ending 're-enactment',[6] mainly because it had been conceived as a means to display the experimental efforts to shape a new kind of art history, and, furthermore, had been the result of 'team play'.[7]

3 Ernst H. Gombrich, *Aby Warburg: An Intellectual Biography* (London: Warburg Institute, 1970).

4 See Emily J. Levine, *Hamburg, Dreamland of Humanists: Warburg, Cassirer, Panofsky, and the Hamburg School* (Chicago: University of Chicago Press, 2013).

5 Aby Warburg, *Gesammelte Schriften*, ed. by Ulrich Pfisterer, Horst Bredekamp, Michael Diers, Uwe Fleckner, Michael Thimann, and Claudia Wedepohl (Berlin: Akademie Verlag, 1998–), II.1: *Der Bilderatlas MNEMOSYNE*, ed. by Martin Warnke and Claudia Brink (2000); in Italian as Aby Warburg, *Mnemosyne. L'Atlante delle immagini*, ed. by Maurizio Ghelardi (Turin: Nino Aragno Editore, 2002).

6 Cristina Baldacci and Clio Nicastro, 'Il Bilderatlas Mnemosyne rivisitato: una mostra e un convegno a Karlsruhe', *Engramma. La tradizione classica nella memoria occidentale*, 142 (2017) <http://www.engramma.it/eOS/index.php?id_articolo=3086> [accessed 18 December 2018].

7 Monica Centanni, 'Editoriale: Engramma da 0 a 100', *Engramma*, 100 (2012) <http://www.engramma.it/eOS/index.php?id_articolo=1161> [accessed 18 December 2018].

The dictionary definition of 'renewal' identifies it as 'an instance of resuming something after an interruption' or 'the replacement or repair of something'. To renew, thus, is to give fresh life or strength to something. As part of the second meaning, 'recovery' is listed as one of the synonyms for renewal. This link between 'renewal' and 'recovery' erratically leads me to the core of Warburg's unique method, both by following the intertwined threads that bind the different fields of research he explored and combined, and by delving into a crucial event in his life. However, one should always keep in mind Edgard Wind's methodological suggestion in his biting review of Gombrich's Warburg biography. Here, Wind, criticizing Gombrich's statement about the possibility of understanding Warburg's work only if one gets lost in his maze, warns the scholar approaching the enormous number of Warburg's notes and drafts that these 'fragments' have to be considered as no more than preparatory scribbles.[8] They constitute an essential part of Warburg's work, but they also need to be contextualized within a broader frame.

Warburg's fresh and crucial contribution to rethinking the implications of Renaissance symbolic forms was the result of his radical questioning concerning the migration of artistic forms in space and time. With this objective, he conferred a pivotal role to the materiality of mediatic supports and took into account all those secondary objects that at the beginning of the twentieth century were mostly overlooked by art historians, as, for instance, the tools of daily life, tapestry, or coins.

8 'He was like a man lost in a maze and the reader who attempts the next chapter should perhaps be warned that he, too, will have to enter the maze.' Edgar Wind, 'On a Recent Biography of Warburg', in *The Eloquence of Symbols. Studies in Humanistic Art*, ed. by Jaynie Anderson (Oxford: Oxford University Press, 1983), pp. 106–13.

The art objects, which for such an expansive conception cannot, thus, be reduced to their aesthetic qualities, are here conceived as vessels, as symptoms of the intricacy of human multi-layered temporality, made of interruptions, resumptions, inversions, regressions, stops, and accelerations. Warburg recognized in the artistic crystallization of expressive gestures and forms the physical embodiment of this ungraspable and discontinuous fluctuation of time. The renewal of different symbolic meanings emerges from apparently identical elements and styles, yet unpredictably awakes something that had not previously been there, that is, what Warburg called 'dynamogram', a term borrowed from biology, more precisely from Richard Semon's *The Mneme.*[9] In this book from 1904, Semon uses the term 'engram' to name the traces of events on the living organism's nervous system and he provides an explanation of how these energies can be reactivated when the organism encounters new experiences at a later point.

By reframing Semon's notion within his theory of the image, Warburg conceives of 'dynamograms' as crystallizations of the images of ancient psychic energies surviving in the form of an inherited memory, which are renewed only through the contact with a new epoch, in the overturning or energetic inversion of the original meaning.[10] Organic and inorganic time — what Andrea Pinotti poignantly calls memories of the neutral[11] — mingle in this immobilized time, the trace of events guarded by art objects that disclose the world of possibilities held in the past as a result of the collision between *Pathosformeln* (forms of pathos)

9 Richard Semon, *Die Mneme als erhaltendes Princip im Wechsel des organischen Geschehens* (Leipzig: Engelmann, 1904).

10 Ernst Gombrich, *Aby Warburg*, p. 248.

11 Andrea Pinotti, *Memorie del neutro. Morfologia dell'immagine in Aby Warburg* (Milan: Mimesis, 2001).

and *Nachleben* (survivals). Warburg's ultimate project was to rewrite (with words and images) the history of art as a history of the passions, avoiding the most obvious and partial conception of progress as a linear, teleological succession of ages.

Today, Warburg's idea of art history has perhaps begun to sound familiar, yet certainly no less timely, even current, as it exemplifies, for instance, a particularly radical approach to interdisciplinary research and resonates with the rise of interest in affect theory. In this respect, the unsolvable contradictions that feature both in Warburg's personality (what he fondly called his 'Janus face') and in his work, provide the probably most intriguing aspects to inquire into. 'Du lebst und thust mir nichts',[12] you live and do me no harm, is one of the best-known Warburgian mottos. He uses it to describe the safe space of experience that only art can create, as it is the unique human dimension where the polarity between the rational and the irrational finds a temporary reconciliation in what he calls *Denkraum der Besonnenheit*, the thinking-space of reflection ('sophrosyne').

In the draft for his essay from 1920, 'Pagan-Antique Prophecy in Words and Images in the Age of Luther',[13] Warburg defines the *Denkraum* as a *Zeitspanne*, the time span between stimulus and response that characterizes human perception. As a devoted reader of Nietzsche and Burckhardt (not to mention his friend Ernst Cassirer),

12 Aby Warburg, *Grundlegende Bruchstücke zu einer pragmatischen Ausdruckskunde. Frammenti sull'espressione*, ed. by Susanne Müller (Pisa: Edizioni della Normale, 2011). The fragments have since been re-edited in Warburg, *Gesammelte Schriften*, IV: *Fragmente zur Ausdruckskunde*, ed. by Ulrich Pfisterer and Hans Christian Hönes (2015).

13 Aby Warburg, 'Pagan-Antique Prophecy in Words and Images in the Age of Luther', in *The Renewal of Pagan Antiquity*, pp. 597–697.

he aimed to overcome the opposition between Apollonian and Dionysian principles: Warburg remained sceptical with respect to excess and at the same time cultivated access to the passions through symbolic forms. The Warburgian *Denkraum,* hence, is conceived not as a utopian condition of balance and accord, but a force field of unpolarized, that is, reversible irrational and rational energies that can take shape only through contact with the 'other'.

Warburg's obsession with maintaining the right distance from reality in order to avoid the risk of incorporation, 'to recompose the fracture between man and the outside world'[14] seems to be the leitmotif of his entire life. In 1921, after several failed attempts in other psychiatric institutions and right after his last violent crisis when he threatened his relatives with a revolver, Warburg was admitted to Bellevue, whose director at the time was Ludwig Binswanger, who subsequently became Warburg's psychiatrist. His diagnosis was schizophrenia, but it was later revised by Emil Kraepelin, who considered the case a 'mixed-state manic-depressive'. Against all expectation, during the three-year therapy at Bellevue, Warburg was able to slowly restore connections with family and colleagues, first of all Fritz Saxl, who provided crucial support in the preparation of his famous and controversial lecture *The Ritual of the Snake.*[15] The story of Warburg's Kreuzlingen lecture is well-known and has become almost legendary; his presentation in front of the doctors and the patients of Bellevue is indeed

---

14 Filippo Trentin, 'Warburg's Ghost: On Literary Atlases and the 'Anatopic' Shift of a Cartographic Object', in *De/Constituting Wholes: Towards Partiality Without Parts,* ed. by Manuele Gragnolati and Christoph F. E. Holzhey (Vienna: Turia + Kant, 2017), pp. 101–29 (p. 122).

15 Aby Warburg, 'A Lecture on Serpent Ritual', *Journal of the Warburg Institute,* 2 (1938–39), pp. 222–92.

often described as a turning point in Warburg's healing journey. Recovery, though, is rarely a peak but rather a process, and what we actually find at stake in this lecture is precisely the peculiar temporality of symbolic renewal. By focussing on the material he had collected in 1896/1897, during the period he conducted field research in the villages of the American Hopi, Warburg's lecture sheds light on one of his primary interests, namely the psychic parallelism between the movement of an individual's life (for instance in mimicry) and the style of artistic movement. The journey in Arizona and in New Mexico had provided him with the opportunity to search in Hopi ritual practices for the stylistic forces shaping moving life into art that he had discerned in Renaissance symbolic forms. Behind and beyond their aesthetic-formal value, images embody the human biological need to shape and express the vital as well as historical development of the passions.

Hence Warburg's conception of an image-engram does not arrest or in any way pacify the constitutive instability, the pulsating movement it captures between the energetic poles of human conflict, namely the oscillation between primitive and chaotic energies and the rational faculty to organize the world. His personal experience, as well as his investigation of the Renaissance, tell us something about the necessary 'interruption' implied both in 'renewal' and 'recovery'. Renewal is not synonymous with 'rebirth', the latter being often associated with the Renaissance in contrast to the Middle Ages. Rebirth requires having been dead and being born a second time in a different body. In the case of renewal, however, the body is the same, and it carries the more or less conspicuous traces of the familiar symptoms. Interruptions are not always visible, they are not always tragic and neat marks, they can be 'just' one of the shapes of time — as well as one way to deal with time.

Repetition

DANIEL REEVE

The Simpsons, the world's best-known animated sitcom, has a curious relation to time, as everyone who has seen it knows.[1] In any given episode, a remarkable sequence of events takes place: Bart may win an elephant in a radio phone-in competition,[2] or Homer may become the owner of the Denver Broncos as a result of the generosity of his supervillain boss,[3] or Lisa may give a principled speech that results in the arrest of a corrupt politician).[4] And yet the consequences of these life-changing happenings do not survive beyond the end of the episode in which they take place: the credits roll, the reset button is pushed, and the family returns to their sofa.[5] At the beginning of each new

1 *The Simpsons*, created by Matt Groening (Fox Broadcasting, 1989–).

2 'Bart Gets an Elephant', season 5, episode 17, dir. by Jim Reardon (aired 16 January 1994).

3 'You Only Move Twice', season 8, episode 2, dir. by Mike Anderson (aired 3 November 1996).

4 'Mr. Lisa Goes to Washington', season 3, episode 2, dir. by Wes Archer (aired 26 September 1991).

5 There is one major exception: the two-part episode 'Who Shot Mr. Burns?', season 6, episode 25, dir. by Jeffrey Lynch (aired 21 May 1995), and season 7, episode 1, dir. by Wes Archer (aired 17 September 1995).

episode, we are invited to forget the years of accreted narrative that precedes it, except when these accretions are played for laughs.[6] Episode breaks thus function as a way of regenerating a state of near-endless potential for new stories, unencumbered by the need for continuity. This state of potential is maintained equally by another strange temporality. We know that *The Simpsons* takes place in a universe in which time passes. The show frequently depicts flashbacks to the characters' younger selves (notably, Homer's sung recollection of his life as a beer-seeking seventeen-year-old in 'Duffless'[7]), or flash-forwards to older versions of its protagonists (Bart as a good-for nothing divorcee, and Lisa as a successful businesswoman, in 'Holidays of Future Passed'[8]). However, none of the characters have aged in the main narrative sequence since the beginning of the show's run in 1989. True, the present-day time in which the show takes place has moved forward in pace with the production date of each episode — so an episode first aired in 2002 is understood as taking place roughly at that time — but the overall effect of this presentness is to sharpen further this sense of stasis. We should not understand *The Simpsons* as existing within historical time; instead, the show's situatedness in a roughly present time should be taken as a guarantee that it is *not* historically placed. The show exists inside historical time, but isolated from its flow. I want to suggest that we must understand the events of *The Simpsons* taking place, impossibly, within

---

6 For instance, the exchange between Bart and Lisa in 'The Two Mrs. Nahasapeemapetilons', season 9, episode 7, dir. by Steven Dean Moore (aired 16 November 1997): '— I wish I had an elephant! — You did. His name was Stampy. You loved him. — Oh, yeah.'

7 'Duffless', season 4, episode 16, dir. by Jim Reardon (aired 18 February 1993).

8 'Holidays of Future Passed', season 23, episode 9, dir. by Rob Oliver (aired 11 December 2011).

the span of a single year — one in which Bart is ten, Lisa eight, and so on; and one which exists within a timeless, ahistorical present approximated by the vague nowness of the show's setting. This is, of course, a ridiculous thing to say about a text that does not require narrative or temporal consistency to function effectively as a piece of entertainment, but I want to insist on it for the time being.

The commercial benefits of the distinctive temporality outlined above are difficult to overstate. Long-running serial texts that depend on visible human performers have to contend with the fact that these performers tend to age and change out of pace with the text. Actors may die, quit, or otherwise change in such a way that they are no longer able to perform the role as written, and jarring, immersion-breaking means must be employed to explain their absence or altered appearance. *The Simpsons,* because it is animated, can operate over a much longer arc: it has a much greater capacity to convincingly reset itself (and, in doing so, to renew its potential for producing narrative) than live-action serial television. The show's attitude towards time solves, perhaps more successfully than any other work of television, the contradictory demands of serial textuality: the demand for innovation, for new stories, alongside the need for a stasis that guarantees recognizability and consistency.

A paradox emerges: to maximize the possibility of continued commercial success, a serially extended text must stay the same — stay recognizably itself, true to the core of its own original appeal — as its run continues through time. At the same time it must change, because of the demand for new stories within the established formulas, and because of an expectation that each iteration produce a sense of closure. Such texts must therefore change as little as possible; they must satisfy a need for new stories while remaining, in quite a strong sense, themselves. The temporal oddities of *The Simpsons* are, I suggest, explicable as a response to these practical demands. *The Simpsons* is perhaps the exemplary case of a text that has, by means of these strategies, successfully ensured its own extended continuation, even in the face of the (widely acknowledged) declining quality of its writing.

Some observations follow from the above: (1) Human finitude presents a constant challenge to serial textuality, especially in a commercial situation that demands the extended reproduction of a profitable textual product, which must ideally remain self-similar in order to ensure its continued success. (2) Serial texts must nevertheless generate an impression of novelty, change or progress with respect to their prior iterations: total stasis is not an option. (3) Certain temporal strategies, as exemplified by *The Simpsons,* provide a space in which a middle ground between finitude and stasis can emerge. (4) The concept of seriality that emerges from this examination is one of pure iteration; one in which no element of a series exists in a consequential (i.e., historical) relation with another.

At this point I would like to return to the point made above about the impossibly capacious year in which the events of *The Simpsons* appear to take place, since this show is not the first serial cultural product to be established in a period of time set apart from the flow of history, both infinitely accommodating and firmly constrained. In the middle of the twelfth century, the Jersey poet Wace writes a history of the British people in octosyllabic couplets, beginning with the story of the founder of Britain, the exiled Trojan prince Brutus. The poem narrates Brutus's discovery of Britain, up to that point empty apart from a few giants (lines 1063–64), and recounts the deeds of successive kings of

Britain up to the end of their domination of the British Isles with the death of King Arthur. An important passage for the purposes of this essay comes in the middle of Arthur's reign, after his consolidation of power across the British Isles, but before his final and hubristic campaign of imperial conquest. Wace tells us that twelve years of peace elapsed between these two periods of historically significant events. He says:

> For twelve years after his return, Arthur reigned in peace. No one dared to make war on him, nor did he go to war himself. [...] In this time of great peace I speak of — I do not know if you have heard of it — the wondrous events appeared and the adventures were sought out which, whether for love of his generosity, or for fear of his bravery, are so often told about Arthur that they have become the stuff of fiction: not all lies, not all truth, neither total folly nor total wisdom. The raconteurs have told so many yarns, the story-tellers so many stories, to embellish their tales that they have made it all appear fiction.[9]

This moment has been thought of as an origin story for medieval romance, a fictional narrative mode that recounts exactly the kind of fantastic adventures that Wace describes

---

9 Wace, *Roman de Brut: A History of the British*, ed. and trans. by Judith Weiss, rev. edn, Exeter Medieval Texts and Studies (Liverpool: Liverpool University Press, 2002), lines 9731–34, 9785–99: 'Duze ans puis cel repairement / Regna Artur paisiblement, / Ne nuls guerreier ne l'osa / Ne il altre ne guereia. [...] Que pur amur de sa largesce, / Que pur poür de sa prüesce, / En cele grant pais ke jo di, / Ne sai si vus l'avez oï, / Furent les merveilles pruvees / E les aventures truvees / Ki d'Artur sunt tant recuntees / Ke a fable sunt aturnees: / Ne tut mençunge, ne tut veir / Ne tut folie ne tut saveir. / Tant unt li cunteür cunté / E li fableür tant flablé / Pur lur cuntes enbeleter, / Que tut unt fait fable sembler.'

here.[10] But, perhaps more importantly, we might note that these fictions come into being — perhaps fiction in general comes into being — by means of a temporal constraint. By retreating from historical time, with its necessary depiction of human finitude, fiction initiates the possibility of the infinite multiplication of incident within a single constrained temporal frame — Wace's twelve years of romance, or the single year of *The Simpsons*.

Though medieval romances were written by many different authors, I want to suggest that these texts nevertheless deploy similar strategies of generic self-perpetuation, markedly distinct from the standard self-referential gesture of historiographical writing in this period, which justifies the writing of new historical narratives by claiming that the new text is more accurate, or more complete, than all of its now-obsolete predecessors. Romance makes no such claim: it does not need to because of the infinite capacity of the twelve years in which all these texts (at least symbolically) take place. What romances do instead is reset themselves by means of a kind of return: each text ends where it began, with an originally disrupted stasis restored, and hence with the endless possibility of new disruptions and challenges, whether these will be faced by the original protagonist, his son, or another hero entirely.[11] As in the case of *The Simpsons*, this is seriality as pure iteration. No one element exists in a historical or consequential relation with any other; historical time expands sideways to accommodate endlessly iterable narrative.

---

10 See Dennis H. Green, *The Beginnings of Medieval Romance: Fact and Fiction, 1150–1220* (Cambridge: Cambridge University Press, 2002), p. 192; and Ad Putter, 'Finding Time for Romance: Mediaeval Arthurian Literary History', *Medium Aevum* 63 (1994), pp. 1–16.

11 The protagonists of medieval romance are (almost without exception) gendered male.

I have argued that such a temporality involves definite commercial advantages in the case of *The Simpsons*, and the same is true of romance, which responds in its own way to the same problem of innovative stasis navigated by the form of the serial animated sitcom. Audiences demand novelty even as their tastes remain conservative. The temporal constraint of fiction represents a compromise between stasis and innovation; one which may have been prompted at various points in cultural history by a material need to produce a reliably consumable serial product. Emerging from this need, fiction instigates a mode of repetition distinct from both the bare repetition of sameness and purely formal repetition, which divides linear time into regular units irrespective of content. This mode of repetition contains the potential for infinite reproduction, endless self-similarity, but unlike the bare repetition of sameness, remains comprehensible within human frameworks of desire and politics by separating end from conclusion.[12]

12 On the politics of time, see Christiane Frey, 'Restrain'; for a sequel to this essay, see Daniel Reeve, 'Resolution', (both in this volume).

Repetition

Differential Monotony, Affects, Creation

ARIANNA SFORZINI

The notion of repetition has been variously analysed in twentieth-century philosophy as a means to question the concepts of representation and mimesis together with the traditional ideas of the subject and object of knowledge. Michel Foucault, Gilles Deleuze, Jacques Derrida — among others — are the main philosophers who conceived of a new relation between history, subjectivity, and reality in which 'repetition' and its 'difference' are at stake. The Foucauldian reactivation of the Deleuzean concept of repetition as 'difference without a concept' is particularly interesting as it allows to approach this contemporary debate about the gesture of repeating — reaffirming a double which is never a simple copy of an original element. In order to describe this philosophical use of the notion of repetition, however, it is important to recall another central twentieth-century conceptualization of the repetition mechanisms that could be usefully described as an 'other repetition' in relation to which Foucault (the most Deleuzean Foucault) elaborates his thought: the Freudian repetition according to Freud's fundamental 1920 *Beyond the Pleasure Principle.*[1]

In this text, Freud questions his own theory insofar as it took the pursuit of pleasure as the only force regulating the behaviour of living organisms. Anyone would instinctively look for pleasure and avoid pain. Yet the observation of various patients showing strange compulsive behaviours convinced Freud that there must be something 'beyond' the simple principle of pleasure. Individuals often engage in repetitions of gestures or thoughts that are clearly painful, far from being a source of gratification. How is it even possible to fixate on a traumatic experience? Shouldn't the mind stick to pleasant memories and forget hurtful ones, as far as it can? *Beyond the Pleasure Principle* is largely influenced by the spread of post-traumatic disorders, which were a painful reality in 1920 Europe, in the immediate aftermath of the World War I. These traumatic neuroses were believed to derive from physical injuries the soldiers sustained during the war. But Freud proposed another theory. He observed that the post-traumatic symptoms were common even among people who hadn't been physically wounded, indeed even among the civilian population, despite the fact that they hadn't witnessed the war first hand. Some patients seemed 'traumatized' by their own fantasies and desires.

What strikes Freud in post-traumatic neuroses is precisely these patients' compulsion to repeat traumatic ex-

1 Sigmund Freud, *Beyond the Pleasure Principle* [1920], in *The Standard Edition of the Complete Psychological Works of Sigmund Freud*, ed. and trans. by James Strachey, 24 vols (London: Hogarth, 1953–74), XVIII: *Beyond the Pleasure Principle, Group Psychology and Other Works (1920–22)* (1955), pp. 1–64.

periences, for example, by dreaming of them. Why should the unconscious mind re-propose images and feelings that have been traumatic for the individual? Freud himself had previously considered dreams as the symbolic expression of unconscious desires — for instance in his seminal 1900 work on the interpretation of dreams.[2] He thought the unconscious mind uses dreams to fulfil its own desires even if they go against social constraints. Nightmares, however, are difficult to explain with this analytical pattern. After traumatic experiences, bad dreams tend to activate the trauma itself indefinitely, despite the individual's conscious efforts to drive the mind away from it.

Oddly enough, Freud finds a possible answer to this repetition compulsion by analysing a children's game. He famously termed it the '*Fort-Da*' experience: he observes his 18-months-old grandson, Ernst, repeatedly throwing away a toy and picking it up again, while repeating the expression '*fort-da*' ('gone' and 'there'). Freud affirms that the child's behaviour is not guided by the principle of pleasure — by any kind of immediate self-satisfaction. The point of the *Fort-Da* is the repetition itself, or more precisely, the compulsion of repeating a particular traumatic experience: the mother leaving the child, the child's realization of the necessity of being separated from the mother. The repetition is a means of mastering a trauma in an active and creative way: the child is attempting to deal with a situation it couldn't foresee and which is definitely out of its control. More generally, following Freud, any trauma then presents itself as a feeling the individual couldn't anticipate nor expect — for example through anxiety — and that she is obliged to master through its repetition, even if this re-

2 Sigmund Freud, *The Interpretation of Dreams* [1900], in *The Standard Edition*, IV–V (1953).

peating action is a source of displeasure. Repetition is the compulsive return of a past the individual couldn't anticipate. It embodies a non-linear temporality the individual mind has to reproduce in order to master an affective and potentially disruptive energy. The repetition is a sort of 'technique of the self' more or less effective to make oneself survive one's own traumatic past.

The Foucauldian notion of repetition, re-enacting Deleuze's philosophy, implicitly refers to the Freudian one, but does so in order to distort and reverse it. The repetition put into play by Foucault has three main characteristics: (1) It is de-psychologized, acting on the level of discourse and not in the depth of the human mind; (2) It is affectively de-individualizing, dissolving the individual subject into a complex and heterogeneous web of anonymous relations; (3) It is temporally erratic, using the power of a senseless repetition not to provide a meaning to a traumatic past experience but to create a new space of future possibility. The repetition is not the reactivation of the *same*, from past to present, but the interruptive monotony of the *different*, from present to future.

'Repetition' is explicitly mentioned by Foucault in two texts he wrote on Deleuze's books *Difference and Repetition* and *The Logic of Sense*: 'Ariane s'est pendue' (1969) and *Theatrum philosophicum* (1970).[3] It reactivates an-

3 Gilles Deleuze, *Difference and Repetition* [1968], trans. by Paul R. Patton (New York: Columbia University Press, 1994); *The Logic of Sense* [1969], trans. by M. Lester with C. Stivale (New York: Columbia University Press, 1990). Michel Foucault, 'Ariane s'est pendue' [1969], in Foucault, *Dits et écrits*, ed. by Daniel Defert, François Ewald, and Jacques Lagrange, 2 vols (Paris: Gallimard, 2001), I: *1954–1975*, text n° 64, pp. 795–99; 'Theatrum philosophicum' [1970], trans. by Donald F. Brouchard and Sherry Simon, in *Essential Works of Foucault, 1954–1984*, ed. by Paul Rabinow, 3 vols (New York: New Press, 1998–2001),

other very important notion in Foucault's early works on discourse published in the 1960s: the *double*. The double is a peculiar attribute of discourse and of literature in particular. Literary language in general is for Foucault at the same time defective and excessive: defective because words are rare compared to things and language is irreducible to the real world; excessive because, in their autonomy from reality, words can become an instrument of freedom, transforming our attitude towards the world and inventing new forms of being, unexpected possibilities of thought and existence. The double is a name for this experience of freedom by means of literary language. Literature is a series of doubles, of 'doppelgängers', of mimes of reality whose role is not to truthfully represent reality itself but to modify it through its multiple repetitions, its heterogeneous reflections in a distorting mirror. The position of a double for Foucault is never that of a reproduction of an original model but the dispersion of the very idea of an 'origin' of sense through the indefinite re-proposition of its copies. The double is not the *same* nor the *other* of the *same*, but something new and irreducible in its own difference.

Foucault gives many examples of this literary repetition: the stupidity of Flaubert's *Bouvard and Pécuchet*, Sade and his almost boring descriptions of sex and violence, the 'mises en abyme' of Baroque theatre, the stories Sheherazade tells to escape death in *One Thousand and One Nights*, Raymond Roussel's *jeux de mots*, the surrealist poems, and many others. And yet, the most famous and probably the most intuitive examples of repetition as the emergence of difference are pictorial ones: Magritte's

---

II: *Aesthetics, Method, and Epistemology*, ed. by James D. Faubion (1998), pp. 343–68.

works (in his renowned text 'This Is Not a Pipe')[4] and Andy Warhol pop series. To take the example of his account of Warhol's *Campbell's Soup Cans*, produced in 1962: the same soup can is repeated 32 times, and it is precisely this apparently senseless repetition that allows for difference to arise as the minimal and yet fundamental fracture in the uniform space of meanings and values:

> This is the greatness of Warhol with his canned foods, senseless accidents, and his series of advertising smiles: the oral and nutritional equivalence of those half-open lips, teeth, tomato sauce, that hygiene based on detergents; the equivalence of death in the cavity of an eviscerated car, at the top of a telephone pole and at the end of a wire, and between the glistening, steel blue arms of the electric chair. 'It's the same either way,' stupidity says, while sinking into itself and infinitely extending its nature with the things it says of itself; 'Here or there, it's always the same thing; what difference if the colours vary, if they're darker or lighter. It's all so senseless — life, women, death! How stupid this stupidity!' But, in concentrating on this boundless monotony, we find the sudden illumination of multiplicity itself — with nothing at its centre, at its highest point, or beyond it — a flickering of light that travels even faster than the eyes and successively lights up the moving labels and the captive snapshots that refer to each other to eternity, without ever saying anything: suddenly, arising from the background of the old inertia of equivalences, the zebra stripe of the event tears through the darkness, and the eternal phantasm informs that soup can, that singular and depthless face.[5]

4 Michel Foucault, *This Is Not a Pipe* [1968], trans. by J. Harkness (Berkeley: University of California Press, 1983).

5 Foucault, 'Theatrum philosophicum', p. 362.

In an unpublished text on Andy Warhol's *Marilyn Diptych* (1962), Foucault affirms that the series of Marilyns are a sort of deformed doppelgänger of the classical '*tableau*', the diptych of the title and its series: the series of images are not 'serialized' in order to classify, master, hierarchize, and unify them.[6] Rather, the 'series of series' composed by the repetition of Marilyn's smile, is a 'difference of differences': a 'savage multiplicity', the repetition of difference, the difference of repetition.

There is, then, a 'repetition compulsion' in the Foucauldian philosophical practice. But it does not correspond to the psychological need to master a traumatic past in order to build a meaningful individual subjectivity. It is, on the contrary, the power of breaking the uniform sets of values that shape our present and the present forms of discourse and individualities. It is the immense possibility of rupture that resides in any minimal difference repeated through the minute, tiny gestures of art, language, but also everyday lives. There is always another time within time, another possible world to create, hidden between the monotony of repetition and its differences.

6 Michel Foucault Archives, Bibliothèque nationale de France, boîte 53, (NAF 28730).

Repetition

TOM VANDEPUTTE

Is there a concept of repetition? Can repetition be defined clearly, can it be delimited without ambiguity? Can this word, 'repetition', be made to correspond to a concept that is both univocal and stable — a concept that can be iterated again, at another time or place, without difference or alteration? Is there, in other words, a concept of repetition that is *repeatable*? Does such a concept not already presuppose an understanding of what it is yet to grasp? Does it not anticipate the meaning of a word it is yet to define? Has the concept of repetition — and with it every concept — not already proposed that repetition is indeed possible? And has it not already determined this repetition as a repetition of a certain kind — a repetition whose content remains stable and constant, a repetition of one and the same thing, a repetition without alteration? Has one, then, not already spoken of repetition before one has even begun to define it?

These questions form the background to a remark that is found in the writings of Johann Georg Hamann — a contemporary and close friend of Kant, whose critique of pure reason was the most important target of Hamann's later polemical writings. In an important passage from a letter of 1769 included in the third volume of his collected writings, we read:

> There are thoughts that one has only once in one's life and which one is not able to produce again [*Gedanken [...] die man nur Einmal in seinem Leben hat, und nicht Meister ist wieder hervorzubringen*].[1]

As an astute reader of Hamann has noted, it is however this thought — precisely this thought — that occurs again in the fifth volume of his collected writings, in a letter composed several years later, in 1773.[2] Here we read:

> It seems to me that there are certain thoughts we are only able to have once in our life [*daß wir gewißer Gedanken nur einmal in unserem Leben fähig sind*].[3]

Es giebt Gedanken, we read, *gewiße Gedanken,* certain thoughts — but exactly which thoughts are referred to here? Is this merely a reflection on some thoughts and not others, on a specific class of thoughts that only occur once? *Es giebt Gedanken die man nur Einmal in seinem Leben hat,* Hamann writes. What if this remark is read as a reflection on a much broader class of thoughts than it seems to describe at first sight — on the thoughts of finite, human beings as distinct from divine thought? *Es giebt*

1 Johann Georg Hamann, *Schriften*, ed. Friedrich Roth, 7 vols (Berlin: Riemer, 1821–25), III (1822), p. 392.

2 Søren Kierkegaard, *Søren Kierkegaards Skrifter elektronisk version 1.8.1*, ed. by Karsten Kynde (Copenhagen: Søren Kierkegaard Forsknings-centeret, 2014), 'Journaler og papirer', DD:28 <http://www.sks.dk/DD/txt.xml> [accessed 16 December 2018].

3 Hamann, *Schriften*, v (1824), p. 25.

Gedanken die man nur Einmal in seinem Leben hat, und nicht Meister ist wieder hervorzubringen. That certain thoughts occur only once, thus, does not seem to be an accident: we think these thoughts only once, writes Hamann, because we are not able to think them again. We are not able to think them again because we do not have absolute mastery over our thoughts; we do not relate to them as a master relates to a servant who can be commanded at will. There would seem to be a force that inheres in these thoughts that impedes our ability to master them, to produce them again at our own will, a dynamic by virtue of which such thoughts are unrepeatable — at least for finite beings.

How this unrepeatability is to be understood is not specified in the remark. That is to say, it is not *stated* here. The remark does not say anything about this impossibility of repeating certain thoughts; it does, however, engage in a repetition itself. Yet it is not immediately clear whether this repetition illustrates the assertion, whether it demonstrates it 'silently' — just as Diogenes countered the Eleatic denial of motion by simply pacing back and forth a few times. At first, it may seem as if Hamann's repeated iteration of this thought does precisely the opposite of what it states — if, at least, the statement is taken to refer to the unrepeatability of the thoughts of finite, human beings as opposed to those of a divine being. Is the thought that is put forward here not the same as before? Is it not one and the same thought that is produced here once again? The fact that the second iteration does not use the exact same words only seems to support this. Does Hamann not say the same thing — only in different words? The differences between the two iterations — the substitution of *man* by *uns*, of *es giebt Gedanken* by *gewisse Gedanken* — can easily be understood as paraphrasing one and the same thought.

The same can be said about the replacement of *Gedanken haben und hervorbringen* in the first iteration and *Gedanken fähig sein* in the second. Is this not merely a paraphrase, a summary with the same semantic content?

Indeed, the comical effect of the two sentences depends precisely on the fact that they can be read as repeated iterations of one and the same thought — the thought that certain thoughts cannot be repeated. If these two sentences would not appear as iterations of the same thought, they would not appear to contradict what they state. And yet at the same time, the repetition complicates the possibility to understand the two remarks as repetitions of one and the same thought. When this same thought is iterated once again, its meaning seems to have shifted. Not that one meaning would have been replaced by another; the repetition of the thought that certain thoughts cannot be repeated rather calls into question whether it means anything at all. Once it is repeated, what is meant in the first iteration no longer seems to be quite so stable: insofar as it appears to contradict itself, it is, suddenly, permeated by the possibility of irony.

This irony is difficult to curtail. Not only is it no longer certain what is meant, it is also uncertain whether it is even possible to decide with certainty whether there is an irony here at all. The possibility of irony first opens up when one perceives a contradiction between the semantic content of the sentence and its repetition. But is it even certain that there is a contradiction? Is it certain that this thought is one of those thoughts that the remark refers to? And is it even certain that this is a repetition of one and the same thought? Or does Hamann, in the second letter, speak of a thought that is quite different from the first? Is it merely an accident that the same words — *Gedanken, Einmal* —

appear here once more? Even the instability of the remark is difficult to determine in a stable way.

The repetition of this thought, of one and the same thought, does not leave it intact. It is not that the alteration of meaning affects only the second iteration; it is not that the second iteration means something different because it has already been said while the first iteration still means the same. The alteration does not only affect the second iteration; it does not leave the meaning of the first iteration intact. What is meant in the first iteration dissolves. It becomes impossible to read this iteration if it is not already read in relation to its double. Likewise, the second iteration has no stable meaning on its own. It becomes possible to read only in relation to the first. The repetition thus not only destabilizes the meaning of the thought but also its unity. It turns out not to be possible to speak of one and the same thought that would be stated twice; the thought — what is supposedly meant by what is said — is never one but already two. It is not a repeated thought, but a thought that is always already a repetition. Hamann's remark thus turns out to be far from a statement on the unicity of thought, a simple assertion of its irreducible *Einmaligkeit*. At the same time as it speaks of the unrepeatability of thought, it conjures up a thought that is constituted only in and as repetition.

Resistance I

HANNAH PROCTOR

1937 — Hitler is ensconced at the Reichstag, Stalinist terror reigns in Moscow and the Republican Army are battling the fascists in Spain. In Berlin, a group of young communists gaze at the ancient battle of deities and giants depicted on the Pergamon Altar. This is how Peter Weiss begins his epic three-volume novel *The Aesthetics of Resistance*. Sinewy stone figures wrestle in a state of petrified unrest, their heroic actions frozen *in media res*. The scene is 'shattered into fragments'. 'Yawning cracks' cut once whole figures to pieces. Muscular stumps, bits of jaw, leg, ankle, and 'tremendous and dismembered hands' protrude from the hard marble.[1] Hands without fingers, shoulders without arms, fists without swords... Mutilated bodies strangle, clamber and clutch at one another desperately. Torsos convulse in pain. Ligaments tear, sweat pours, blood congeals, arteries swell. The silence, occasionally broken by the soft echoes of tourists' footsteps, seems

1 Peter Weiss, *The Aesthetics of Resistance, Volume 1: A Novel*, trans. by Joachim Neugroschel (Durham, NC: Duke University Press, 2005), pp. 3–5.

to contain an 'inaudible roaring' that the young observers strain to hear:[2]

> We heard the thuds of the clubs, the shrilling whistles, the moans, the splashing of blood. We looked back at a prehistoric past, and for an instant the prospect of the future likewise filled up with a massacre impenetrable to the thought of liberation.[3]

They gaze at the beaten and the dying. They stare at the stone and it is as though they can see their own future defeats unfold before their eyes, brutal defeats that the novel goes on to trace in visceral detail. 'The silence, the paralysis of those fated to be trampled into the ground continued to be palpable.'[4] But they perceive other struggles contained in the panorama of devastation. The scene is one of antagonism and striving rather than of resignation; perhaps another outcome could have been possible. The scene also seems to function as a possible source of hope and spur to resistance, confirming the necessity to keep on fighting.

The Aesthetics of Resistance itself stands as a scarred monument to past struggles. Weiss is unflinching in his portrayal of political failure and the historical wreckage of twentieth-century Europe. Yet, as Fredric Jameson discusses, he is concerned with asking 'how to draw energy from such endless images of horror'.[5] Forced to contemplate the novel's corpse-strewn pages, Weiss places the reader in the position of his young protagonists at the Pergamon Altar in order to provide 'a lesson about the

---

2 Ibid., pp. 3–5.

3 Ibid., p. 9.

4 Ibid.

5 Fredric Jameson, 'Foreword: A Monument to Radical Instants', in Weiss, *The Aesthetics of Resistance*, pp. vii–xlix (p. xliii).

productive uses of a past and a history that is not simply represented or commemorated but also reappropriated by some new future of our own present'.[6] The novel ends by returning to the frieze, dwelling on the empty space on the altar where the lion's paw of Heracles should be: 'The empty space in the frieze, at the spot where the lion's paw of Heracles would hang, designates precisely something absent, unrealized.'[7] The empty space is left open for future intervention. As Weiss himself stated, both the Pergamon and his novel are addressed to the present: 'that turmoil, those figures tangled up in relentless, dreadful combat, figures strangling one another, lacerating one another with spears. It is the very same struggle that we are engaged in today.'[8]

The novel's narrative ends in 1945 but was written decades later. Weiss died in 1982, shortly after the publication of the novel's third and final volume (the first having appeared in 1975). The Berlin wall fell seven years after that, bringing to an end one of the major conflicts that animates the narrative: between the official positions (both political and aesthetic) of the Communist Party and unorthodox communist idealism. This conflict is also evident in Weiss's play *Trotsky in Exile,* which points to a gap between historical materialist predictions and historical reality as it unfolded. A programme note by Ernest Mandel written to accompany a production of the play in London remarks:

---

6 Ibid., p. xlvii.

7 Klaus R. Scherpe and James Gussen, 'Reading the *Aesthetics of Resistance*: Ten Working Theses', *New German Critique,* 30 (Autumn 1983), pp. 97–105 (p. 104).

8 Burkhardt Lindner and Christian Rogowski, 'Between Pergamon and Plötzensee: Another Way of Depicting the Course of Events an Interview with Peter Weiss', *New German Critique,* 30 (Autumn 1983), pp. 107–26 (p. 120).

> The theoretical controversies, which initiate the play — concerning the role of the peasant, the proletariat, the intelligentsia and the bourgeoisie in the coming Russian revolution, the precise, future form of government and society, the organizations of revolutionaries most appropriate to a rapid success — all find at most a contradictory, incomplete or provisional validation in the actual course of history.[9]

Weiss stages theoretical discussions against the backdrop of historical events that surge weirdly and wildly in directions that the protagonists cannot predict and thus constantly destabilize, undermine, or complicate their pronouncements; theory and praxis (or perhaps it would make more sense to say ideas and history) crash into each other constantly. Jameson's description of *The Aesthetics of Resistance* is also pertinent here: 'the urgency of the dialogical [...] is fueled by a passion for a unity that can never come into being.'[10] The passion for unity that the text exhibits is rooted in a relation to an orthodox Marxist-Leninist understanding of the dialectical movement of history, which sees tensions resolve in a final moment of reconciliation (Absolute Knowledge/Communism). Weiss does not operate entirely within the parameters of this paradigm but whether consciously or unconsciously, critically or obediently, he nonetheless contends with the dominant Party line.

Jameson's discussion of dialogism in Weiss invokes the Soviet literary scholar Mikhail Bakhtin, who argued that language is always internally split. Bakhtin acknowledged

---

9 Ernest Mandel, 'Trotsky in Exile' [programme notes from the 1971 London production] <https://www.marxists.org/archive/mandel/1971/xx/exile.htm> [accessed 20 December 2018].

10 Jameson, 'Foreword', p. xxvii.

that language is 'ideologically saturated',[11] but claimed that the apparently rigid structures of the 'unitary language' always operate in the midst of heteroglossia;[12] a tendency to unite is constantly undermined by a tendency to disassemble. The unitary language and heteroglossia are in constant dialogue; the former imposing limits, tending towards stasis and ossification, the latter always fighting to resist these constraints. The unitary language is centripetal, it keeps the language moving uniformly along a prescribed path, whereas heteroglossia is centrifugal; it pulls things apart. For Bakhtin, every utterance is 'a contradiction-ridden, tension-filled unity of two embattled tendencies in the life of language'.[13] This tension between these two modes of language recalls the tension between a particular meta-historical understanding of progressive time and the messiness of history as it unfolded in practice.

In an essay reflecting on Weiss's work, W. G. Sebald perceives a similar tension in a self-portrait of Weiss, which demonstrates 'both the will to resist and a process that may be described as the assimilation of the chill of the system which the subject knows threatens him.'[14] The work operates within a particular ideologically saturated discourse, which the experiences being described cannot be fully contained by. Heteroglossia — although it would be clearer to

11 Mikhail Bakhtin, 'Discourse in the Novel', in *The Dialogic Imagination: Four Essays*, ed. by Michael Holquist, trans. by Michael Holquist and Caryl Emerson (Austin: University of Texas Press, 1981), pp. 259–422 (p. 271).

12 The Russian term is '*raznorechiye*', derived from '*ravno*' (different) and '*rechi*' (speech).

13 Bakhtin, 'Discourse in the Novel', p. 272.

14 W. G. Sebald, 'The Remorse of the Heart: On Memory and Cruelty in the Work of Peter Weiss', *On the Natural History of Destruction*, trans. by Anthea Bell (New York: Random House, 2003), pp. 169–91 (p. 175).

say history — intrudes, cracking open the official unitary language.

The second volume of *The Aesthetics of Resistance* contains a long meditation on Théodore Géricault's painting *The Raft of Medusa* (1818-19). Weiss's fascination doesn't only concern the painting itself, which displays the splayed corpses of the drowned shipwreck victims (and could in some sense be aligned with the Pergamon Altar), but also Géricault's personal and embodied sufferings — how the artist's struggle became intertwined with his subject matter in some sense. And as Weiss's novel unfolds, it similarly reflects this damaged subjectivity. As Sebald observes: 'the grotesque deformities of our inner lives have their background and origin in collective social history'.[15]

Is it possible for a damaged subject to damage the damaging world? Can individuals resolve their internal fractures through collective action? In Weiss's work the extent to which people are capable of changing or intervening in the course of that history remains a fraught question. In Weiss's 1963 play *Marat/Sade* (or *The Persecution and Assassination of Jean-Paul Marat as Performed by the Inmates of the Asylum of Charenton Under the Direction of the Marquis de Sade*), the tension between history and nature (or the contingent and the immutable) is exemplified by the figures of Marat and Sade respectively. Sade takes the position that nature is a 'passionless spectator'[16] indifferent to humanity, declaring that

> Nature herself would watch unmoved
> if we destroyed the entire human race.[17]

15 Ibid., p. 184.

16 Peter Weiss, *Marat/Sade*, trans. by Geoffrey Skelton and Adrian Mitchell (New York; Atheneum, 1983), p. 23.

17 Ibid., p. 24.

Marat, on the other hand, insists on the possibility of intervention:

> Against Nature's silence I use action
> In the vast indifference I invent a meaning
> I don't watch unmoved I intervene
> and say that this and this are wrong
> and I work to alter them and improve them
> The important thing
> is to pull yourself up by your own hair
> to turn yourself inside out
> and see the whole world with fresh eyes.[18]

The play stages rather than resolves this contradiction. Structured as a play-within-a-play performed by patients in an asylum, *Marat/Sade* is set in 1808; the revolutionary events that are directed by Sade and performed by the inmates (which culminate in the assassination of Marat) took place in the preceding years. In addition to the dynamic between Sade and Marat there is also a tension between the patients and hospital workers. If the asylum is understood as a microcosm of France then this distinction between the insane and the sane maps onto a class antagonism between the proletariat and the bourgeoisie. The patients, ordinary French people who have not benefitted from the revolution, come into constant conflict with the bourgeois people who run the hospital, setting up a conflict-ridden dialogue similar to the relation between heteroglossia and unitary language. Weiss also aligns the Parisian audience of Sade's play-within-a-play with the contemporary audience he is addressing. According to John J. White, Weiss's depiction of French history, which draws a parallel between Marat and Sade should be

18 Ibid., p. 27.

read as a comment on German history, drawing an analogous connection between the Nazi past and the West German present. For White the pronouncements of Sade regarding the immutability of history are characteristic of the play as a whole, which is governed by a 'cruel note of historical determinism'; history becomes a play lunatics are forced to perform like puppets.[19] This seems to offer a bleaker view of the world than the opening scene in *The Aesthetics of Resistance.* Would it be possible to imagine a scenario in which the audience somehow prises open a space for intervention, refuses the seemingly mechanically repetitious cycles history is fatefully trapped in to refuse the 'chill of the system'? Could the asylum's inmates overturn their situation in the manner dreamed of by the young protagonists standing before the Pergamon Altar?

Weiss's works pose often unresolvable questions about the relationships between writing and action, aesthetics and politics. They suggest that only through reckoning with the wounds of history can wounded subjects produced by history resist the continued perpetration of future violence.

19 John J. White, 'History and Cruelty in Peter Weiss's "Marat/Sade"', *Modern Language Review*, 63.2 (1968), pp. 437–48 (p. 447).

Resistance II

HANNAH PROCTOR

> The air is alive with the possibilities of assembling, gathering, congregating. At any moment, the promise of insurrection, the miracle of upheaval; small groups... and strangers threaten to become an ensemble, to incite treason en masse.
>
> Saidiya Hartman, 'The Terrible Beauty of the Slum'

The summer I moved to Berlin I read *The Many Headed Hydra* by Peter Linebaugh and Marcus Rediker. The book is a rousing work of 'history from below' that criss-crosses the Atlantic, charting rebellions, rebellious movements, and the movement of rebellious ideas that emerged with the expansion of trade and colonization in the early seventeenth century. The 'hydra' was a pejorative term used by the ruling classes to describe the new motley groups and collectivities that attended capitalist expansion.[1] As I read

1 Peter Linebaugh and Marcus Rediker, *The Many-Headed Hydra: Sailors, Slaves, Commoners, and the Hidden History of the Revolutionary Atlantic* (Boston: Beacon, 2013).

the book I created a list of the groups, subjects, and figures that the authors mention. These are the hydra's very many heads detached from their contexts of struggle to create a giant amorphous mass. In reading this list out loud I was intrigued by what effect the sheer proliferation might produce — if it might capture something of the possibilities of 'assembling, gathering, congregating' that Hartman describes or whether it rather slips into fatigue or meaninglessness. I'm also interested in what some of the somewhat anachronistic professions or descriptions of groups might mean when thought in relation to on-going struggles in the present. Could the list be constantly expanded?

dispossessed commoners, transported felons, indentured servants, religious radicals, pirates, urban labourers, soldiers, sailors, African slaves

rogues and beggars
entertainers, sex workers
the chapmen, the tinkers, the peddlers
the discharged or wounded
The entertainers of the day — the jugglers, fencers, minstrels, keepers of dancing bears, athletes, and players of interludes
fortune-tellers
all those outside of organized wage labour
swarms of idle persons
peoples who lived without property, work, masters, or kings
many different kinds of people, with many different kinds of work experience: sailors, labourers, craftsmen, and commoners of several sorts, including Native Americans
a motley crew
the amorphous labouring class
hewers of wood and drawers of water
spade men, brick men, carpenters

the dispossessed, the strangers, the women, the children
orphans, vagrants, petty offenders, disorderly women
The Gypsies
the radical protestant, the sturdy rogue, the redundant craftsman, the Catholic recusant, the wild Irishman, the commonist, and the cutpurse
heretics and thieves
servants and fugitives of many languages and colours
the lumpenproletariat
the proletariat
the land rovers
all those who rejected wage labour: the Abraham-men, palliards, clapperdudgeons, whipjacks, dummerers, files, dunakers, cursitors, Roberds-men, swadlers, prigs, anglers, fraters, rufflers, bawdy-baskets, autem-morts, walking morts, doxies, and dells
assassins, Amazons, Anabaptists
religious radicals, indigenous Americans, Africans, commoners
the vagabonds, the master-less
mechanics, watermen, apprentices
the lowly and the base
the Levellers and the Diggers
the urban rioters and the rural commoners
The Ranters
the witches
sailors, clowns, mechanics, and radical sectaries
roarers, ranters, swearers, and bell-ringers
antinomians
mechanic preachers
independent women
West Indians
market gardeners, and river workers such as the watermen, ferrymen, and fishermen
market women, carters, porters, sailors, weavers,

silk winders, and all the other poor discontented persons
Tribeless, landless, nameless,
Wealthless, hostless, fameless
the sailor of the European deep-sea ship and the boatman of the African canoe
a multilinguistic, multiethnic crew
mutineers
Quakers
renegades
European and African American slaves (with and without indentures), felons, landless paupers, beggars, pirates, and rebels of all kinds
London Levellers, Irish soldiers, Barbadian servants, and Virginia slaves
saltwater vagabonds
coopers, gunners, sailmakers
outcasts of all nations
the convicts, prostitutes, debtors
men of unfortunate and desperate condition
peasant rebels, demobilized soldiers, dispossessed smallholders, unemployed workers
Brethren of the Coast
banditti of all nations
a mix't multitude
cross-dressing female warriors
the outcasts of the nations of the earth
arsonists
the dispossessed of all colours [who] feasted, danced, sang, took oaths, and planned their resistance
obscure people with no visible way of subsistence
a mass of desperate but necessarily creative proletarians being forced to work for wages
the Papa, from the Slave Coast near Whydah; the Igbo, from the area around the Niger River; and the Malagasay, from Madagascar
Shamans of Gold Coast origins
haters of the Army
rioters

Afro-Hispanic sailors
radical itinerants
heretics
conspirators
maroons
whalemen
a mini-diaspora
malefactors
rogues
insurgents
mobs
agitators and organisers
the most degenerated, and abandoned
scum and dregs
outcasts
malcontents
gangs of the tobacco and sugar plantations
armed agglomerations
refugees, boat people, evacuees, and prisoners
strikers
hoisters of the red flag
sons of Jamaica
runaways
a motley rabble of saucy boys
wretches, with tethered garments
traitors
the vanguard
Turbulent people of all Nations engaged in illicit
Trade
the disenfranchised
shoemakers, hatters, clockmakers
visionaries
dockers
friends and comrades
mass cultivators of the soil
avengers
the oppressed
multiethnic gangs of labourers
housekeepers, lovers, and nurses
freedom fighters
sappers, miners, pick and shovel workers

the half-clothed and the half-drunk
the volatile and the frolicsome
castaways
millenarian dissidents
ignorant turtlers
Sheffield cutlers
an injured and exasperated people
artisans, Jacobins, Jews
heterodox thinkers
abolitionists
the vanquished
lunatics
agrarian communists
poor disinherited earth worms
jack tars, coal-heavers, dustmen, women of colour, old and young
the factory worker
food rioters; army agitators; barbarians of the commons
aquatic labourers, free thinkers and striking textile workers
the forgotten, the utopian
multitudinous, numerous, and growing
numbered, weighed, and measured
cooperative and labouring
motley vulgar planetary
self-active, creative
Alive

Resistance

TOM VANDEPUTTE

Resist: from the Latin *re-sistere*. Literally: to stand again — that is to say, to cease one's movement, to remain standing, to stand still. This literal sense of the word, *resistere* as a cessation of movement, informs its ancient usage. One of the most common uses of the Latin verb is in the imperative, *resiste*: the demand to 'halt' or 'stop'. The verb is also used figuratively to indicate a cessation of the movement of speech itself: *resistere media in voce*, to stop in the middle of saying something.

What does it mean to think resistance in the modern, political sense of the word in light of its etymological root? What does it mean to think resistance not as a play of force and counterforce, of action and reaction, but rather in terms of movement and its arrest? What does it mean to think of resistance, *Widerstand*, in terms of standstill, *Stillstand*?

These questions are a persistent concern in the work of Walter Benjamin. Benjamin uses the word *Widerstand* only rarely. But when the word does surface in his writings, it is deployed as a technical term at the nexus of his political thought and his reflections on history. What constitutes resistance in its political dimension is perhaps best captured by a formula that is found in a study of the early 1920s, where Benjamin refers to 'a resistance against the stream of historical becoming' (*ein Widerstand gegen den [...] Strom geschichtlichen Werdens*).[1] This resistance is not directed against one process of becoming and in favour of another. Rather it is a resistance against historical becoming as such — history insofar as it manifests itself as a stream, a continuous flow.

Nowhere does Benjamin elaborate what is entailed in such resistance more clearly than in his work on Karl Kraus. His essay on the Viennese journalist, Benjamin writes in a notebook, is to 'designate the place, where I stand and do not participate' (*wo ich stehe und nicht mitmache*).[2] This description of what is at stake in the essay resonates with the first published portrait of Kraus, written in the mid-1920s under the title 'Monument for a warrior' (*Kriegerdenkmal*). Here Benjamin conjures up an image of the writer as an ancient warrior caught up in a battle against a force that constantly threatens to overpower him. The adjectives punctuating the portrait evoke a fight that must appear to be already lost: his struggles against his contemporaries are 'hopeless'; his attempts to change the world are 'helpless';

---

1 Walter Benjamin, '"El mayor monstruo, los celos" von Calderón und "Herodes und Mariamne" von Hebbel. Bemerkungen zum Problem des historischen Dramas', in *Gesammelte Schriften*, ed. by Rolf Tiedemann and Hermann Schweppenhäuser, 7 vols (Frankfurt a.M.: Suhrkamp, 1972–91) II: *Aufsätze, Essays, Vorträge* (1977), pp. 246–76 (p. 249). [Benjamin's *Gesammelte Schriften* will henceforth be abbreviated as *GS*. All translations are mine.]

2 Walter Benjamin, 'Schemata zu "Karl Kraus" <1>', in *GS* II: pp. 1091–94 (p. 1093).

his humanity is 'powerless'. 'The rock with which he is to bury his enemy rolls out of his hands as it did for Sisyphus'.[3]

For the force against which Kraus never ceases to struggle despite this powerlessness Benjamin reserves the name 'world history' (*Weltgeschichte*). Kraus is the emblematic figure of an experience of the history of the world that never loses sight of its catastrophic dimension. In the writings of Kraus, perhaps most notably 'The Last Days of Mankind', Benjamin recognizes the insight that the catastrophe is neither an exception in history nor some event that still awaits us; the real catastrophe is that the world — *this* world — continues to run its course. Or, as a careful reader of Benjamin has paraphrased this thesis: 'The continuum — continuation as such — is the catastrophe'.[4] This experience of history is marked by a curious inversion of the concept of progress (*Fortschritt*) and the corresponding representation of a progression (*Fortschreiten*) of humankind through time. The advancement of history is not conceived as humankind's steady approach towards its moral destination; rather, the very progression of history, its *Fortschreiten*, is grasped as the inexorable perpetuation of misery and suffering. 'The concept of progress is to be founded in the idea of catastrophe', Benjamin writes; 'that things "go on like this" *is* the catastrophe (*daß es "so weiter" geht, ist die Katastrophe*)'.[5]

In the figure of Kraus, this experience of world history as catastrophe is pushed to an extreme. History congeals

---

3 Benjamin, 'Einbahnstraße', in *GS* IV: *Kleine Prosa, Baudelaire-Übertragungen* (1972), pp. 83–148 (p. 121).

4 Rebecca Comay, 'Benjamin's Endgame', in *Walter Benjamin's Philosophy*, ed. by Andrew Benjamin and Peter Osborne (London: Routledge, 1993), pp. 251–91.

5 Benjamin, 'Zentralpark', in *GS* I: *Abhandlungen* (1974), pp. 655–90 (p. 683).

into a concatenation of events and takes its course fatefully, as if it were subjected to laws of nature. 'For him', Benjamin writes, 'the horrible years of his life are not history, but nature: a river, condemned to meander through a landscape of hell'.[6] The 'stream of historical becoming' here returns as a river condemned to take its catastrophic course — an image of the history of a world that has abandoned its hope for divine salvation or the capacity of human beings to change it through purposeful activity. The reference to a 'landscape of hell' evokes the specific temporal structure of this history: hell is here to be understood not in the religious but in the mythical sense, as the ever-renewed, self-same present of Sisyphus Benjamin describes in notes of the same period. The point of ancient representations of hell, writes Benjamin, is not 'that "the same always happens again" [...] but that the face of the world, its enormous head, does not change precisely in what is newest, that this "newest" always remains the same.'[7]

Just as the experience of the progression of history undergoes an inversion, so the corresponding concept of the political is turned inside out. If there is a political dimension to Kraus's writings, it can only begin from his resistance to the advance of this catastrophic history — not as a positive contribution to the progression of humankind towards its moral destination. To the a priori will described by Kant, the will for the 'highest good' that discloses the task to promote its realization in a 'moral community', Benjamin counterposes another will: 'the will to interrupt the course of the world' (*der tiefste Wille [...] den Weltlauf zu unterbrechen*).[8] If the Kantian political will is directed to-

6 Benjamin, 'Karl Kraus', in *GS* II, pp. 335–67 (p. 341).

7 Benjamin, *GS* V: *Das Passagen-Werk* (1982), pp. 1010–11.

8 Benjamin, 'Zentralpark' [*GS* I], p. 667.

wards an ever-receding but positive telos, this will intends nothing but a cessation.

A model for this will — which Benjamin describes in the same fragment as 'the will of Joshua' — is found in the 'idiosyncrasy' (*die Idiosynkrasie*), Kraus's 'highest critical organ'.[9] Benjamin uses this term in the precise medical sense of an excessive physical reaction to something; the sense that is preserved in the German, where the terms can be used to describe the intolerance towards a certain sound, taste, or other sensation — the paradigmatic example being the intolerance for the sound of a nail scratching the surface of a blackboard. The idiosyncrasy thus exemplifies a will without positive end, a pure negativity: a state of extreme intolerance towards a phenomenon, where one cannot bear that it continues and is entirely preoccupied by the desire for it to stop. That Benjamin describes the 'will to interrupt the course of the world' as 'the will of Joshua' — the biblical figure who prayed that God help the Israelites in their battles at Gibeon by making the sun stand still — suggests that this desire is to be understood first and foremost in temporal terms. Towards the end of the essay, in a crucial passage, Benjamin cites one of Kraus's poems:

> Let time stand still! Sun, you come to completion! / Make the end great! Announce eternity! / [...] You golden bell, melt in your own heat, / become a cannon against the cosmic foe![10]

'Let time stand still (*Lasse stehen die Zeit*)' — the will for history to be interrupted in its course is here described as a demand for time itself to be brought to a stop. The

9 Benjamin, 'Karl Kraus' [*GS* II], p. 346.

10 Ibid., p. 365.

resistance against the course of history that manifests itself as a 'stream of becoming' is rendered here as a resistance against time — that is to say, against time that manifests itself as a continuous flow. The impossible demand that Kraus makes is, in other words, a demand for the cessation of the flowing time in which the time that passes is not differentiated from a time that is yet to come; it is a demand that has no positive aim but arises from the *Widerstand* and *Widersinn*, a resistance that is also a repugnance at a flowing time in which every past and future are merely modifications of an ever-same present.

The resistance against time that is figured here thus has nothing to do with a desire for endurance — quite the contrary. What is unbearable about the flow of time is not that things do not endure, that everything perishes in time, but rather that the world and its time remain the same in this passing and coming into being. That Kraus, as portrayed by Benjamin, cannot stand time means that he cannot stand *this* time, the continuum — or what is described here as the time of the sun, the 'cosmic foe' that comes and goes day after day, again and again. It is this 'golden bell' that Kraus demands to melt in its own heat: rather than a desire for persistence, this demand for standstill would arise out of a desire for time as such to perish.

Resolution

DANIEL REEVE

The classic family sitcom characteristically builds resolution into its 22-minute structure. Each episode sets up a moralizing conclusion in which one or more characters learn something — for example, to trust a loved one, or to take a step towards a longer-term personal change. But this mechanism is cynical because genuine progress is inimical to the genre's episodic form.[1] If a sitcom is premised on its main characters having certain flaws (and they almost universally are), then any attempt to address those flaws outside the arc of a single episode is a departure from what made the show interesting in the first place. These mechanisms become frequently parodied, though never fully superseded, in later works — from *Seinfeld*, with Larry David's much-quoted refusal to allow the show's characters any personal development whatsoever ('No hugging. No learning.'), to the recent Netflix animated drama *Bojack Horseman*.[2] In this show, the eponymous main character is the former star of *Horsin' Around*, a saccharine

1 See Daniel Reeve, 'Repetition', in this volume.

2 *Seinfeld*, created by Larry David and Jerry Seinfeld (NBC, 1989–1998); *Bojack Horseman*, created by Raphael Bob-Waksberg (Netflix, 2014–).

90s family sitcom recognizable as a parody of the popular ABC sitcom *Full House.*[3] We meet Bojack in 2014: a depressed figure, who has barely worked since his sitcom's cancellation twenty years earlier, he compulsively rewatches his own show, obsessed with the possibility of satisfying closure, and imagines its credit reel rolling in front of his eyes whenever he experiences a moment of insight or personal growth. But *Bojack Horseman* itself expresses a violent structural opposition to the possibility of episodic resolution. One of the ways in which it does this is through an intense commitment to continuity between episodes. During an alcoholic blackout, Bojack steals the 'D' from the Hollywood sign (season 1, episode 6), and in all subsequent episodes the show's characters universally refer to the neighbourhood as 'Hollywoo', even as the major narrative repercussions of Bojack's theft fade away. Minor details persist determinedly through entire seasons — Bojack hits a deer with his car (season 2, episode 4), and his broken windscreen persists stubbornly through several episode breaks.[4] Training montages decay into distraction or hopelessness, refusing to make the hard work of self-improvement easier by means of temporal manipulation. The message is clear: resolution is not easily achieved; things remain broken. Nevertheless, despite the show's remarkable willingness to follow this committed refusal of resolution into disturbing plots involving abuse, irrevers-

3 *Full House*, created by Jeff Franklin (ABC, 1987–1995).

4 Compare this with a telling moment in *The Simpsons*, created by Matt Groening (Fox Broadcasting, 1989–), 'Bart vs. Australia', season 6, episode 16, dir. by Wes Archer (aired on 19 February 1995), in which a clump of Bart's hair is shaved away by a boomerang, only to regrow apparently within seconds. This moment should not be regarded as simply an animator's continuity error, but rather as a reminder of how certain kinds of continuity and consequentiality are unimportant to the cultural project of *The Simpsons*.

ible cruelty, and the deaths of major characters, *Bojack Horseman* cannot function without signalling — perhaps even despite itself — at least the possibility of resolution over a longer arc by means of the redemption of its protagonist. Though the show offers a sharp, perceptive parody of the 22-minute resolution arc of the family sitcom, demonstrating the unsustainability of such a form when continuity of character and consequentiality of action are prioritized, we might ask whether the parody brings us any closer to a concept of resolution freed from all formal constraints. The repetitive satisfaction of the family sitcom is in a sense a deferral of any genuinely satisfying satisfaction, the deferral of a conclusive end. Seen in this light, *Bojack Horseman*'s refusal of resolution begins to look very similar to the family sitcom's use of 'fake' closure as a structuring principle. Moreover, perhaps *Bojack Horseman*'s rejection of episodic resolution misses the point, since it is so difficult to imagine a narrative text that could ever successfully refuse resolution in any strong sense: all narratives are finite (because they are specific), and as such have endings — endings to which meaning inevitably accrues. Even the most arbitrary endings imaginable — for example, those that occur on account of authorial death or abandonment — are easily, perhaps even inevitably, absorbed into discourses of resolution. In one of the most famous examples of inconclusive textuality, the final piece in Johann Sebastian Bach's monumental work *The Art of Fugue* (*Die Kunst der Fuge*) trails off unfinished, and in doing so leaves incomplete the tonal, rhetorical, and structural schemes of the piece, as well as the entire work. A note added by Bach's son in the autograph manuscript gravely informs the reader that 'over this fugue, where the name BACH is stated in the countersubject, the author died.'[5] Loose ends are subsumed unavoidably into structures of meaning, whether by processes of commentary or extension. Today, performers of Bach's fugue either rely on speculative reconstructions of the piece's final synthesis of its themes, or solemnly enact its incomplete ending, but whether the piece stands as a monument to intricate schematism or a stark reminder of the hubristic danger of such projects, resolution — which I am beginning to define as the retrospective determination of the shape, and hence the meaning, of a textual iteration — is inescapable.

Bojack Horseman expresses a tension between, on the one hand, the recognition of the cynicism inherent in narrative structures of resolution, and on the other, what I claim is the impossibility of ever abandoning such structures. One of the great (yet largely uncelebrated) poems of the Middle Ages, Hue of Rotelande's *Ipomedon*, also explores the contradictions and difficulties involved in taking a position against resolution. In this work, written in England towards the end of the twelfth century, we are told about the deeds of the eponymous Ipomedon, a great knight, in fact the greatest in the world, who falls in love with a beautiful woman known as La Fiere (The Proud One). Because La Fiere is proud, she will only marry the best knight in the world, and we know that this is Ipomedon. However, La Fiere does not know this, because Ipomedon pretends to be a dandy, feigning a lack of interest in all courtly pursuits apart from hunting. La Fiere,

5 Staatsbibliothek zu Berlin, MS Mus. ms. autogr. Bach P200/1, fascicle 3, p. 39: 'Ueber dieser Fuge, wo der Nahme B A C H im Contrasubject angebracht worden, ist der Verfaßer gestorben'. <https://www.bach-digital.de/rsc/viewer/BachDigitalSource_derivate_00062812/db_bachp0200-1_page039.jpg> [accessed 8 December 2018].

under pressure to find a husband who meets her stringent criteria, organizes a three-day tournament in which all of the best knights in the world will compete for the honour of marrying her. Ipomedon, for reasons that are never explained, decides to compete in a series of three different disguises, while pretending that he is out hunting instead of participating in the tournament. Ipomedon, in his various disguises, is victorious on each of the three days, and eventually reveals himself. La Fiere thus agrees to marry him — but Ipomedon decides, again, for reasons that are never explained, to continue his adventures across Europe for another three thousand lines, before finally marrying La Fiere at the very end of the poem.[6]

Ipomedon's structural peculiarity, its extended deferral of its own end, has a parodic force: one of the conceits of the text is to recognize that romances are much longer than they need to be, if romances are understood as texts which set up the conditions under which the best knight can marry the most beautiful woman. Ipomedon is the best knight in the world from the beginning of the poem, and could very quickly prove himself to be so. The text could therefore itself end very quickly with marriage and the promised reproduction of aristocratic virtue in the form of children. But *Ipomedon* is a very long text, and so too are romances generally. So, romance, a narrative mode in which very little happens in a certain sense of the word, must resort to narrative strategies of self-prolongation, whether

6 For the text of the poem, see *Ipomedon, poème de Hue de Rotelande*, ed. by A. J. Holden (Paris: Klincksieck, 1979). For a reading of *Ipomedon* that illuminates some aspects of my argument further, see Daniel Reeve, 'Queer Arts of Failure in Hue of Rotelande and Alan of Lille', in *Medieval Thought Experiments: Poetry, Hypothesis, and Experience in the European Middle Ages*, ed. by Philip Knox, Jonathan Morton, and Daniel Reeve (Turnhout: Brepols, 2018), pp. 273–96.

these might be the graphic and detailed description of battles, or subplots only minimally consequential with respect to the broader narrative. *Ipomedon*'s parodic insight is to extend this self-prolongation in order to produce a text that is manifestly too long, and gleefully aware of being so.

Ipomedon ends with an elaborate allegorical conclusion in which an authorial voice appears to claim that the poem's perverse excesses are both exceptionally faithful to the demands of the narrative form of romance and to the desires of its audience. Baked into this accusation is of course a recognition that the poem's parody of romance operates by being, in a certain sense, a maximally successful one — one that extends a minimum amount of narrative material into a poem of nearly eleven thousand lines. *Ipomedon* recognizes that even its own scathing parody cannot avoid the resolution that it so compulsively and mockingly defers. Instead of showing us a romance without resolution, the parody is achieved by altering the balance of the text, the scale at which its structural features play out, in order to create a disproportionate monster.

The question remains: does scale make a difference? For the musicologist Robert Fink, it does. Fink's analysis of twentieth-century American minimal music alongside its historical contemporary and stylistic sibling disco produces an insight into the relationship between repetition and teleology (or resolution).[7] Rejecting previous analyses of minimal music as being radically anti-teleological,[8] Fink proposes instead a concept of

7 Robert Fink, *Repeating Ourselves: American Minimal Music as Cultural Practice* (Berkeley: University of California Press, 2005).

8 The dominant account is that of Wim Mertens, *American Minimal Music*, trans. by J. Hautekiet (New York: Broude, 1983); for a summary of Mertens' claims vis-à-vis musical teleology see Fink, *Repeating Ourselves*, pp. 32–34.

'recombinant teleologies', in which a repetitive musical work performs 'goal-directedness [...] whenever and wherever it chooses; [maintaining] a distance and perhaps even ironic stance toward "traditional" teleological dictates even as it plays with their undeniably pleasurable aspects.'[9] By 'detach[ing] teleology from form',[10] a new way of understanding resolution emerges: not just an inevitable consequence of the punctuating effects of form (though it always remains this), but also a discursive tool capable of being used for any number of purposes.

Seen through a certain analytical lens, this is the move made by *Bojack Horseman*. Working in a form — the episodic animated television comedy — laden with strong expectations that its narrative resolutions will coincide neatly with the end of each episode, *Bojack* offers instead a teleology detached from its form, even if this teleology remains only a provisional rejection or deferral of the inevitable resolution that will accrue to its ending, even though *that* final resolution is, for the time being, a mirage, and remains available, even when enacted, for continuation, extension, and repetition.

This, then, is the 'katechontical' paradox of resolution.[11] All texts, always, are poised to end, and in doing so to perform the finality that is a precise consequence of their finitude. But, on the other hand, time refuses to do anything but carry on, leaving these objects always available for reiteration and continuation.

---

9 Fink, *Repeating Ourselves*, p. 43.

10 Ibid., p. 46.

11 See Christiane Frey, 'Restrain', in this volume, for a discussion of 'katechontical' temporality.

Restrain

CHRISTIANE FREY

The 're-'word this article examines is the verb 'to restrain' — and the nouns derived from it: 'the restrainer' and 'the restraint'. The word stems from the Latin *restringere* and means, first and foremost, 'to hold back', 'to withhold'; it can also mean to 'bind back', to 'put in chains' or figuratively to 'put in limits' or simply 'to limit'. Interestingly enough, the Latin *restringere* can also mean to 'reveal' or 'to lay bare' — for example, a sword (*ferrum*) or one's own hand (*manum*).[1]

What is the particular function of the 're-' in this word? Since both *stringere* and *restringere* denote the action of 'binding', one can indeed pose the question what exactly

1 See the entries on 'restringere' in Gerhard Köbler, *Lateinisches Abkunfts- und Wirkungswörterbuch*, 2nd edn (2009) <http://www.koeblergerhard.de/Latein/LateinischesWB.pdf> [accessed 20 December 2018], p. 1103; Hermann Menge, *Langenscheidts Großwörterbuch Latein*, 2 vols (Berlin: Langenscheidt, 2001), II: *Lateinisch-deutsch, unter Berücksichtigung der Etymologie*, p. 809. — I cannot withhold my gratitude for sustained critique and comments from my co-fellows at the ICI Berlin, as well as from Christoph Holzhey and Arnd Wedemeyer.

the prefix 're-' here contributes. For very obviously, it does not connote a repetition or a restitution — this is not an iterative 're-'. An act of *restringere* does not *stringere* something *again*, nor does it take it *back* to its original status. Rather, the 're-' must be functioning as an intensifier, adding emphasis to the meaning already expressed in the base, *stringere*. Like many Latin prefixes, such as 'ad-', 'ex-', or 'cum-', 're-' can have the function of an aspect marker, signifying 'thoroughness'. 'Resplendent', for example, means not to shine (*splendere*) again or to shine back, but to shine brightly. Similarly, 'to restrain' would thus mean to bind, but to do so thoroughly or fully: perhaps with great intensity, force, or effect.

This way of parsing the word, however, does not yet tell the whole story. The intensifying 're-', here, does not merely strengthen the root meaning while leaving it unchanged; rather, it carries additional connotations, connotations that add to or even alter the meaning of the base. For the intensification of the *stringere* in *restringere* must say something about the *object* of this act of binding. If what is being bound is something that must be *re*strained, *restrictum*, rather than simply *strictum* or bound, then there must be something about it that *calls for* the intensification of the binding signified by the 're-'. If *stringere* points to the simple act of 'tying' or 'binding', re*stringere* would refer, in addition, to the restraint of something that would otherwise, were it not restrained, be in flow, in movement, that is: ongoing. 'To restrain' implies that something that would otherwise continue to perform or execute its force, or move in whatever direction it presses toward, has been arrested. Put differently, the 're-' of *restringere* only makes sense in reference to a force that is being countered, a force that continues to exert itself even if, or even when, it is being prevented from achieving its aim. If there were no force, action, or movement at the outset, there could be no restraint. And one could go still further: the movement or action that is being arrested must be such that it could, potentially, succeed in overcoming the restraining force. If the force being restrained were weak, or of inconsistent direction, the act of restraining would be superfluous. In every restraint, then, there are two forces at work: one that aims, obviously, at continuing its course, or, to say the least, aims at *not* being arrested; and one that arrests, one that suspends — even if intermittently or provisionally — an action or motion. The very 're-' in 'restrain' implies by necessity two different dynamics, or two opposed forces.

The 're-' of the re-strainer thus points to a temporal paradox. The very expression 'to re-strain' necessarily implies *two* times: one, a time that flows forward, and another that arrests, slows or interrupts this forward-flowing time. It thus entails a time and a countertime, a time of flow and a time of halting. The result of the action of *restringere* is a pause, a halting of motion that would otherwise have been relentless. Evidently, the restrainer can therefore only be understood as an anti-teleological figure. The *telos* that is negatively implied in the concept of *restringere* — the *telos* of the movement that has been arrested — is not achieved or at least not yet achieved; it is, on the contrary, prevented, for an indefinite period of time. Now, how are we to understand the time of the restraint? Is it a mere *delay* in the movement that has been arrested — and thus of essentially the same nature as the time that would have been marked out by the movement it prevents? Any chronological description of the process of restraint would force us to see it this way: a (potential) movement has been restrained; just as this movement would have covered a certain distance in a certain span of time, so the delay occupies a span of time, of the very same time in which the movement's progress toward its *telos* could have been measured. In fact, however, if the time of the restraint is of *indefinite* duration, and this is the common sense of 'restrain', then the time of the restraint would seem to be of an entirely different nature than the time of what is being restrained. A restraint is more than a simple delay, a postponement in one and the same time as that occupied by what it postpones. Rather, a restraint interrupts not just a movement but the very time of that movement, in order to institute another kind of time: the indefinite, non-teleological, open-ended time of the restraint. The restraint does not just arrest a movement, but suspends the very time of that movement and imposes its own, essentially different regime of time. Since its duration is indeterminate (the act of restraining could stop after a few seconds or go on for ages), the act of restraining, in other words, gains a certain autarchy.

Of course, in the history of (theo-political) culture, there is a particular concept or figure that points precisely to this 'double-bound' movement: the notorious *katéchon*. The main reference for the many and varied interpretations of this concept is Paul's (or Pseudo-Paul's) Second Epistle to the Thessalonians (2. 6-7). Given its importance and impact on (past and present) theo-political concepts, I will quote it here in its entirety:

> 1 Concerning the coming [*tēs parousias*] of our Lord
> Jesus Christ and our being gathered to him, we ask
> you, brothers and sisters, 2 not to become easily un-
> settled or alarmed by the teaching allegedly from
> us — whether by a prophecy or by word of mouth
> or by letter — asserting that the day of the Lord
> has already come. 3 Don't let anyone deceive you in
> any way, for that day will not come until the rebel-

> lion [*apostasia*] occurs and the man of lawlessness
> is revealed [*kai apokaluphthēi ho anthrōpos tēs ano-*
> *mias*], the man doomed to destruction. [4]He will
> oppose and will exalt himself over everything that
> is called God or is worshiped, so that he sets him-
> self up in God's temple, proclaiming himself to be
> God. [5]Don't you remember that when I was with
> you I used to tell you these things? [6]And now you
> know what is holding him back [*to katechon*], so
> that he may be revealed [*apokaluphthēnai*] at the
> proper time. [7]For the secret power of lawlessness
> [*to mustērion tēs anomias*] is already at work [*en-*
> *ergeitai*]; but the one who now holds it back [*ho*
> *katechōn*] will continue to do so till he is taken out
> of the way. [8]And then the lawless one will be re-
> vealed [*apokaluphthēsetai ho anomos*], whom the
> Lord Jesus will overthrow with the breath of his
> mouth and destroy by the splendor of his coming
> [*tē epiphaneia tēs parousias autou*].[2]

In this passage, the present participle of the verb *katechō* is used, first in the neuter (*to katechon*), then in the masculine (*hō katechōn*). In both cases, its meaning is 'the restrainer': first, it is a *something*, some kind of power that defers, restrains, postpones; and then it is 'the one', 'he' who restrains. Now, what exactly does this 'restrainer' hold back? According to the quoted passage, it is evidently the 'lawlessness', 'the evil' — but that is not all. At the same time that the *katéchon* restrains evil, it/he also keeps it from coming to light (another meaning of the Latin *restringere*).[3] The *katéchon* impedes and postpones *both* the unleashing *and* the revelation of evil, of iniquity. For the revelation of evil occurs only with the second coming of the messiah,

2 Quoted according to *Holy Bible: New International Version* (Colorado Springs: Biblica, 1984). The Greek is transcribed according to *Novum Testamentum Graece*, ed. by Eberhard Nestle, Barbara Aland, and Kurt Aland (Stuttgart: Deutsche Bibelgesellschaft, 2012).

3 See above, fn 1.

the so-called *parousia*. Only when evil is revealed or on the condition that it fully manifests itself, is it in fact destroyed (one of the underlying messages of this passage).[4] And it is in this sense that the *katéchon* must be understood as a Janus-faced figure (just as it is both neuter and masculine in the passage). It holds back the outburst of evil, of chaotic lawlessness, but at the same time it also holds back the revelation and hence the ultimate defeat of evil. The *katéchon* is thus the biblical figure that stands for 'order' (*nomos*) while the 'secret power of lawlessness' (*to mustērion tēs anomias*) is at work. (It should be added, of course, that *nomos* is necessary only because there is *anomias* — and the *anomias* is here not to be confused with grace or any other state that would transcend the *nomos*.)[5] It controls the lawlessness and postpones its unchecked eruption — but it can't overcome it. The final defeat of 'lawlessness' is reserved for the messianic power.

In this very ambiguity lies, I would suggest, the main significance of the *katéchon* as a kind of cultural

---

4 In Revelations 20. 2–3, 7–10, another passage points to the same logic: here we read that the 'ancient serpent', which will have been 'bound' for a 'thousand years', ultimately, at the end of times, 'must be let out for a little while' (the implication being, again, that this will lead to its ultimate destruction).

5 Which is the reading Giorgio Agamben proposes in *The Time That Remains: A Commentary on the Letter to the Romans*, trans. by Patricia Dailey (Stanford: Stanford University Press, 2005). The *katéchon* is a recurrent and clearly central figure in Agamben's writings; see for example: *The Kingdom and the Glory: For a Theological Genealogy of Economy and Government. Homo Sacer II, 4*, trans. by Lorenzo Chiesa (Stanford: Stanford University Press, 2007); *Stasis: Civil War as a Political Paradigm. Homo Sacer II, 2*, trans. by Nicholas Heron (Stanford: Stanford University Press, 2015); *The Mystery of Evil: Benedict XVI and the End of Days*, trans. by Adam Kotsko (Stanford: Stanford University Press, 2017); 'Leviathan's Riddle', in *Leviathans Rätsel*, trans. by Paul Silas Peterson (Tübingen: Mohr Siebeck, 2013); *The Church and the Kingdom*, trans. by Leland de la Durantaye (Chicago: The University of Chicago Press, 2012).

Ur-concept of the double-movement or double-dynamic of *restringere*.[6] And a careful reading of the quoted passage makes clear why, from Hippolytus and Tertullian to Augustin and even to Luther, the *katéchon* at times stands for political order as such, and at other times for the Roman Empire (as the last Empire before the coming of Christ),[7] and at yet other times for both at once: the political order is what controls the power of lawlessness (while chaos and evil brew underneath). Worldly political power thus cannot be condemned — it fulfils a necessary function. At the same time, the political order is not to be confused with the messianic, since the *katéchon*, as good

6 With this I do not mean to imply that the *katéchon* is the *only* 'cultural *Ur*-concept' of the double-dynamic of *restringere*. But it seems to be a particularly prominent and theo-politically charged concept implying two opposing and, also in their temporality, opposed powers.

7 After the disintegration of the Roman Empire, the *katéchon* was identified, for example, with the Empire of Charles the Great and the Holy Roman Empire of the German Nation. The Catholic Church, too, was long believed to fulfil the katechontical function. See among many other contributions to the history of the figure of the *katéchon* and both its temporal and political implications: Carl Schmitt, *The Nomos of the Earth in the International Law of Jus Publicum Europaeum*, trans. by G. L. Ulmen (New York: Telos Press, 2006), pp. 58–70; Wilhelm Stählin, 'Die Gestalt des Antichristen und das "katechon"', in *Festgabe Joseph Lortz*, ed. by Erwin Iserloh and Peter Manns, 2 vols (Baden-Baden: Grimm, 1958), II: *Glaube und Geschichte*, pp. 1–12; G. Meyer, C. Schetter, and J. Prinz, 'Spatial Contestation? The Theological Foundations of Carl Schmitt's Spatial Thought', *Geoforum*, 43 (2012), pp. 687–96; Sergei Prozorov, 'The Katechon in the Age of Biopolitical Nihilism', *Continental Philosophy Review*, 45.4 (2012), pp. 483–505; Felix Grossheutschi, *Carl Schmitt und die Lehre vom Katechon* (Berlin: Duncker & Humblot, 1996); William Rasch, 'Messias oder Katechon? Carl Schmitts Stellung zur politischen Theologie', in *Politische Theologie*, ed. by Jürgen Brokoff and Jürgen Fohrmann (Paderborn: Schöningh, 2003), pp. 39–54; Paul Metzger, *Katechon: II Thess2, 1–12 im Horizont apokalyptischen Denkens* (Berlin: De Gruyter, 2005); Roberto Esposito, *Two: The Machine of Political Theology and the Place of Thought*, trans. by Zakiya Hanafi (New York: Fordham University Press, 2015); Massimo Cacciari, *The Withholding Power: An Essay on Political Theology*, trans. by Edi Pucci (London: Bloomsbury, 2018).

and useful as it/he is in its/his restraining and controlling potency, simultaneously withholds the second coming of Christ, that is, the messianic event. By doing so and by sustaining the state of affairs in which lawlessness may remain concealed, the *katéchon* — that is, for the sake of simplicity, the political order — does not exactly collude with evil, but entertains an alliance with it. It is this particular relationship with evil that renders worldly power, as indispensable as it is, an always already corrupted safeguard against disorder. No salvation and no overcoming of the underlying anomic and chaotic powers can occur within politics. At the same time, there is no doing without politics.

With regards to a particular figure of the restrainer, the power that withholds, the biblical *katéchon,* Roberto Esposito has noted, in his *Immunitas,* that there is an 'aporetic node of life and death, of momentum and restraint, of opening and binding' inherent to the katechontic.[8] The restraining *katéchon* is the principle that, in a way, withholds the coming of the end, thereby postponing death, the ultimate limit or *finis,* or finitude *tout court.* Even if understood independently of the biblical context, one could thus understand the power that restrains at once as a negative force — namely, as a force that withholds movement and action (or drama in the sense of flowing and forward moving action) — and at the same time as a positive force, a force that withholds the end, expiration, death.

My contention is that the 're-' in 'restrain' is what adds to the 'strain', the *stringere,* this aporetic dimension, this double-bind of moving forward and halting, and this double-logic of being at once something one wishes would

8 Roberto Esposito, *Immunitas: The Protection and Negation of Life*, trans. by Zakiya Hanafi (Cambridge: Polity, 2011), p. 57.

prevail and something one wishes would loosen or release to allow the motion to proceed. Restraint always has a double focus — and an ambivalent one at that. It is also my contention that the logic — the paradoxical logic — of the restrainer is deeply ingrained in all processes of life, of drama, of action, of being, and of politics: it is not only the paradox that there is no action without it being at once withheld *and* sustained, but also the ambivalence that it will always remain unclear whether the end being striven for is good or bad. The 're-' of *restringere* thus points to the inherent paradox of representing time as motion, to the inherent 'aporetic node' of the restrainer itself. Read before the backdrop of a long tradition of understanding this aporetic logic of the withholding power in terms of the *katéchon*, the prefix at the same time conveys to what extent diametrically opposed concepts of the political continue to populate the Western imagination. If the 'secular order' or 'worldly government' has the function of withholding *both* the ultimate salvation *and* the final outbreak of chaos, it is unclear whether one should hasten its demise or work for its enduring power. In this line of thought, a sustained — and still outstanding — reflection on the *katéchon* in all its cultural and imaginative ramifications might help to re-strain, this time in the sense of 'to expose', important but, to this day, insufficiently understood dimensions of the political imagination of the West.

Reversion

Lyric Time(s) II

FRANCESCO GIUSTI

In the first of Rainer Maria Rilke's *Duineser Elegien*, *re-citation* occurs both as a poetic principle and as a performed action. What Rilke covertly re-cites is Dante's *Vita nova* (1293–1295). Where can Dante be found in this poem? Some contextual information is needed to become aware of his undisclosed presence. From 22 October 1911 to 9 May 1912, Rilke was a guest of Princess Marie von Thurn und Taxis in the castle of Duino. There Rilke devoted himself to reading the *Vita nova*. The Princess asked the poet to translate Dante's work and he pondered the idea for a while. Eventually, he abandoned the endeavour and, in 1912, started writing the *Duino Elegies* instead. In her memories of Rilke from 1932, the Princess recalls a peculiar episode that occurred while the poet was walking along the cliffs near the castle: 'in the midst of his pondering, he suddenly stopped, for it seemed to him as if a voice had called to him in the roar of the storm.'[1] The voice ap-

1 Marie von Thurn und Taxis-Hohenlohe, *Erinnerungen an Rainer Maria Rilke* (Frankfurt a.M.: Insel, 1994), pp. 48–49. Translations are mine.

parently uttered the following words: 'Who, if I cried out, would hear me among the hierarchies / of angels?' ('Wer, wenn ich schriee, hörte mich denn aus der Engel / Ordnungen?'). [2] Rilke quickly wrote down the sentence in his notebook, and that same evening he drafted the first elegy. The outburst of creativity continued through the following days, when he drafted the second elegy and fragments of later ones. The question heard in the storm came to constitute the opening lines of the poem.

These dynamics of negotiation of poietic agency closely resemble those recounted by Dante in the tenth paragraph (XVIII–XIX) of the *Vita nova*.[3] While walking along a river, Dante the character is suddenly seized by a pressing desire to speak and starts pondering the modality and the potential audience of the speech. At that point,

> [...] my tongue, as if moved of its own accord, spoke and said: *Ladies who have intelligence of love.* With great delight I decided to keep these words in mind and to use them as the beginning of my poem. Later, after returning to the aforementioned city and reflecting for several days, I began writing a canzone, using this beginning, and I constructed it in a way that will appear below in its divisions. The canzone begins: *Ladies who have.*[4]

---

2 All quotations are from Rainer Maria Rilke, *Werke*, ed. by Manfred Engel, Ulrich Fülleborn, Horst Nalewski, and August Stahl, 4 vols. (Frankfurt a.M.: Insel, 1996), II: *Gedichte 1910 bis 1926*, ed. by Manfred Engel and Ulrich Fülleborn, pp. 201–204 (p. 201).Translations are mine.

3 I follow the text and the subdivision of the text into 31 paragraphs provided in Dante Alighieri, *Vita nova*, ed. by Guglielmo Gorni (Turin: Einaudi, 1996). The numbering of the corresponding section in Michele Barbi's edition is provided in Roman numerals in parenthesis.

4 All translations of the *Vita nova* are from Dante Alighieri, *Dante's* Vita Nuova. *New Edition: A Translation and an Essay*, ed. and trans. by Mark Musa (Bloomington: Indiana University Press, 1973). '[...] la mia lingua parlò quasi come per sé stessa mossa e disse: "Donne

The 'origin' of the gesture performed in the opening lines is concealed in Rilke's elegy. Writing literary history, one can retrace it only from contextual information.[5] Why? I would suggest that Rilke knows that this lyric gesture has no proper origin. Receiving verses from external forces is one of the motifs by which the basic gesture of negotiating one's own subjective voice has been traditionally carried out. There is no attempt in the elegy to go back to the 'first' time that gesture was performed in order to repeat it. Even for the presumed first occurrence in the *Vita nova,* one can find a constellation of references spanning from Greek and Latin poetry to numberless recurrences at least up to Valéry's *vers donné*.[6] Rilke's poet-speaker prefers to trace a series of re-enacted gestures with no supersession.

Twenty lines later (26–53), the elegy addresses a 'traditional' condition: the poet is never ready to contain the approaching beloved, the moment of inspiration in its fullness. The movements of thought and expectation seem to divert the poet's attention and make the fullness of experience impossible (whose vocalization is interrupted by the sigh in Dante's 'Tanto gentile e tanto onesta pare'). What, then, could poets do? They should 'sing the lovers' ('singe die Liebenden', l. 36) in order to make their emotions immortal. What kind of song should it be? It should be a song

---

ch'avete intellecto d'amore". Queste parole io ripuosi nella mente con grande letitia, pensando di prenderle per mio cominciamento. Onde poi, ritornato alla sopradecta cittade, pensando alquanti die cominciai una canzone con questo cominciamento, ordinata nel modo che si vedrà di sotto nella sua divisione. La canzone comincia *Donne ch'avete*', in Dante, *Vita nova*, pp. 92–93.

5 For reflections on a possible 'lyric history', see Susan Stewart, 'Preface to a Lyric History', in *The Uses of Literary History*, ed. by Marshall Brown (Durham, NC: Duke University Press, 1996), pp. 199–218.

6 Michel Jarrety, 'The Poetics of Practice and Theory', in *Reading Paul Valéry: Universe in Mind*, ed. by Paul Gifford and Brian Stimpson (Cambridge: Cambridge University Press, 1998), pp. 105–20.

of praise. This praise (*Preisung*) must be constantly started anew, because it is fated never to be fully achieved. Old examples of unfulfilled love should teach 'us' that it is time for 'us' to love without a beloved[7] — one could think of Dante's renunciation of reciprocity in the economy of love, but Beatrice always affects Dante even after her untimely (or too timely) death. This is formulated as an exhortation, or an expectation, addressed to a *you* that might well be the speaker or a future poet. There is no explicit *you* in 'Tanto gentile e tanto onesta pare', but I tried to show in my first contribution ('Recitation') how Dante constructs a text to be shared with potential readers: each monodic vocalization of the poem joins a choral reiteration, somehow de-crystallizing or, in Augustinian terms, distending the distilled 'now' by vocalizing it anew in the present of reading.[8]

Perhaps, this is why Rilke decided not to translate the *Vita nova,* but rather to re-enact it, to take over its way of loving, to inhabit the position of its speaker. In other words, to listen to the 'uninterrupted message' ('die ununterbrochene Nachricht') he mentions in line 60. 'We' should endure, trembling, as 'the arrow endures the bow' ('wie der Pfeil die Sehne besteht', l. 52). It is a matter of recitation more than mere repetition. Re-citation inscribes the renewed gesture and the new self in a long unbroken

7 The plural first person pronoun is used in the poem itself, where the 'I' and the 'you' are included in a 'we' that could be defined by the collective gesture of praise. It seems that different individuals can share this gesture in a form of chorality. Therefore, what can be shared — both synchronically and diachronically — is not a particular object of love, but a certain modality of loving.

8 I am disconnecting here the notions of monodic and choral poetry from their musical accompaniment to engage with their modalities of enunciation. Chorality is crucial to the definition of lyric in W. R. Johnson, *The Idea of Lyric: Lyric Modes in Ancient and Modern Poetry* (Berkeley: University of California Press, 1982).

series whereas repetition instantiates again the old words by appropriating them. In its flight, the arrow is more than itself because of the power the bowstring has given to it, not so much for the target it is directed towards.

So, the trembling song ought to be sung for the power that love exerts, not for an object (the beloved) to be eventually obtained. The relation with objects should not be one of interpretation or attribution of meaning; as Rilke writes at lines 12–13: 'we are not so securely at home / in the interpreted world' ('wir nicht sehr verläßlich zu Haus sind / in der gedeuteten Welt').[9] At the same time, 'we' as humans cannot withstand the angel, and even less embrace a divine being: in fact, if an Angel 'were to suddenly / take me to its heart, I would vanish into its / stronger presence' ('und gesetzt selbst, es nähme / einer mich plötzlich ans Herz: ich verginge von seinem / stärkeren Dasein', ll. 2–4). A different ontological status makes any unmediated contact between human beings and the divine impossible. In a Cavalcantian morbid attitude, this is the effect that the bodily presence of Beatrice has on Dante in the first paragraphs of the *Vita nova*. The vision of her annihilates the last remainders of his vital power: 'not only did the sight of her not defend me: it ultimately annihilated the little life I had left' ('cotal veduta non solamente non mi difendea, ma finalmente disconfiggea la mia poca vita' (9, XVI). However, the angel, as the young dead in the final section of the elegy, can exert some pressure on human beings, can push 'us' toward it. The speaker of the elegies realizes, as much as Dante's speaker, that one cannot fully experience nor

9 See Raoul Walsch, *'daß wir nicht sehr verläßlich zu Haus sind in der gedeuteten Welt': Untersuchung zur Thematik der gedeuteten Welt in Rilkes 'Die Aufzeichnungen des Malte Laurids Brigge', 'Duineser Elegien' und spätester Lyrik* (Würzburg: Königshausen & Neumann, 2012), pp. 226–64.

understand the divine entity; thus a different *relationship*, a new way to *speak* about it, needs to be established.

In rhetoric, reversion — from the Latin *reversio* — denotes all those figures of speech that involve a *turning back*, a *return*, a *coming around again*: anastrophe, chiasmus, epiphora, anaphora. This backward movement, which establishes a present and announces a future, could be transferred from the verbal design of a single poem, through the *œuvre* of an author, to the inner workings of the literary genre.[10] This is another feature that Rilke could find in the *Vita nova*, where Dante attempts to re-cite himself, that is, to assemble old and scattered lyrics turning them into a linear progression towards Christian love and a unitary story of his love for Beatrice. Yet the story ends up being less linear than expected and the linear process of *conversion* to Beatrice is interrupted by *reversions*.[11] An evidence of this problematic is the fact that, as the supposedly teleological narrative proceeds, the new poetic modality — the *stilo della loda* (style of praise) — is not consistently deployed. If the canzone in paragraph 10 (XIX), 'Ladies

10 Riffaterre hints at a similar mechanism: 'It is only in isolation that the poem is difficult and, when made easy, trite. It makes sense only when read as a metonym of the whole genre — like the antique tessera that was just a shard by itself, but a message when fitted to its matching piece. And its significance lies not in hidden depths, but in the fact of its being a variation on a motif', Michael Riffaterre, *Semiotics of Poetry* (Bloomington: Indiana University Press, 1978), p. 163. I argue that the 'variation' does not operate primarily on motifs but rather on gestures. Gestures give form to the speech more than address a thematic content, as *topoi*, motifs, and themes seem to do at different levels. Lyric gestures concern the linguistic practice and show a certain degree of awareness of its limits.

11 According to Harrison, while mourning the death of Beatrice in the sequence of poems composed for the 'donna pietosa', Dante both reverts to previous poetics and explores a different poetic possibility, the 'Petrarchan alternative'. See Robert Pogue Harrison, *The Body of Beatrice* (Baltimore: Johns Hopkins University Press, 1988), pp. 93–109.

who have intelligence of love' ('Donne ch'avete intellecto d'amore'), is ascribed to the new poetics of praise, then the reader has to wait until paragraph 12 (XXI) and then paragraph 17 (XXVI) to have other poems composed in such manner.[12] The poems in-between dangerously revert to previous modalities of loving and poetry writing. Even the poetic supersession that Dante traces in a sort of progressive figural fulfillment is more problematic than sometimes admitted.[13]

Proper praise or *celebration*, in Dante's project, had to be directed toward a specific subject named Beatrice;[14] Rilke retains the *towardness* of the speech but empties the destination. In a certain sense, he prefers the Dante before his definitive conversion (or final reversion) to Beatrice, which is again the outcome first of Beatrice's apparition in

12 The protagonist of the *Vita nova*, Barolini writes, 'does not so much proceed in a consistently forward direction [...] as return again and again to his previous condition, from which he must once more start forth: textual indices of this condition are the *ri* prefix in "*ri*pigliare lo stilo de la sua loda" (XXVI, 4), and the unusual recording of two initial quatrains [...] for the sonnet of chaper XXXIV,' Teodolinda Barolini, '"Cominciandomi dal principio infino a la fine" (*V.N.*, XXIII, 15): Forging Anti-Narrative in the "Vita Nuova"', in *La gloriosa donna de la mente: A Commentary on the* Vita Nuova, ed. by Vincent Moleta (Florence: Olschki, 1994), pp. 119–40 (p. 124).

13 In the *Vita nova*, Dante traces the story of his own poetic development while at the same time outlining a history of recent poetics: from Guittone d'Arezzo and Bonagiunta da Lucca, through Cavalcanti and then Guinizzelli, up to himself. See Zygmunt G. Barański, 'Dante Alighieri: Experimentation and (Self-)Exegesis', in *The Cambridge History of Literary Criticism*, ed. by H. B. Nisbet and Claude Rawson, 9 vols (Cambridge: Cambridge University Press, 1989–), II: *The Middle Ages*, ed. by Alastair Minnis and Ian Johnson (2005), pp. 561–82 (p. 567).

14 Indeed, Dante sees Beatrice 'among the hierarchies of angels', to use Rilke's formulation, first in the vision (*imaginazione*) recounted in 'Donna pietosa e di novella etate' ('A lady of tender years', 14, XXIII) and lastly in the ascension of his spirit to Heaven in 'Oltre la spera che più larga gira' ('Beyond the sphere', 30, XLI). In the final lines of the former, after the vision, he raises his eyes to Heaven and addresses Beatrice directly (ll. 83–84).

a vision and then of Dante's wishful intention. Of course, there is a historical reason for this. In Dante, divine love is granted to the human being: God calls the individual to respond to his love. In Rilke and in modernist negative theology,[15] the angel is utterly removed from all human affairs. In the *Duineser Elegien*, therefore, Rilke problematizes Dante's idea of being called by the other as the driving force of a continuous poetic performance: the response to the request of *conversion* towards the other. He seems rather to propose the intrinsic value of the practice of a perpetual calling upon the silent other: a return to a human position. In the seventh elegy, it is the flow of the summoning voice to keep the angel at a distance: 'Since my call / is always full of effusion, against such a powerful / stream you cannot proceed' ('Denn mein / Anruf ist immer voll Hinweg; wider so starke / Strömung kannst du nicht schreiten', ll. 87–89).[16] This way Rilke seems to revert to a poetics of calling that values the practice of voicing itself — the same poetics on which, according to the first elegy, secular Petrarchism relies in its poetic practice. By mentioning the Italian Renaissance poet Gaspara Stampa, the poem traces its own tradition of lyric subjectivities. They seem to share a long-lasting form of love and a modality of lyric speech that do not expect reciprocation, but are performed by the

15 For a discussion of the role of negative theology in modern and postmodern poetics, see William Franke, *Poetry and Apocalypse: Theological Disclosures of Poetic Language* (Stanford: Stanford University Press, 2009) and *A Philosophy of the Unsayable* (Notre Dame, IN: University of Notre Dame Press, 2014). See also *Languages of the Unsayable: The Play of Negativity in Literature and Literary Theory*, ed. by Sanford Budick and Wolfgang Iser (New York: Columbia University Press, 1989).

16 Rilke, *Werke*, II: pp. 220–23 (p. 223).

poetic effort to appeal to the unattainable entity.[17] The divine is not represented in lyric poetry, it cannot be; rather, poetry embodies the human effort to keep calling.

The lyric poem finds its own place in different temporalities that meet in every act of reading it. The historical form of subjectivity inscribed in a poem can vary according to cultural and historical circumstances, but the discursive mode seems to retain certain gestures that allow for the inscription of subjectivity. Rilke is not *saying* the same words or conveying the same meaning as Dante, he is rather *making* the same gesture under different circumstances and in a different historical context. The lyric as a discursive mode seems to work in a non-linear and non-unidirectional temporality, which is not that of nineteenth-century literary history.

Re-citation is neither intertextuality[18] nor Harold Bloom's agonistic supersession (the 'anxiety of influence'),[19] but rather the effort to reinhabit the position of previous speakers. The lyric poem as a 'script', to use Jonathan Culler's term,[20] could be reconsidered,

---

17 Francesco Giusti, *Il desiderio della lirica. Poesia, creazione, conoscenza* (Rome: Carocci Editore, 2016), pp. 107–09.

18 The phenomenon I am sketching here does not coincide with *intertextuality* as it has been variously defined after Julia Kristeva's use of the term in her 1966 'Word, Dialogue, and Novel', in *Desire in Language: A Semiotic Approach to Literature and Art*, ed. by Leon S. Roudiez, trans. by Thomas Gora, Alice Jardine, and Leon S. Roudiez (New York: Columbia University Press, 1980), pp. 64–91. It neither dissolves the text into a net of other texts nor implies that it is only the reader who gives meaning to the text. *Re-citation*, in the sense I give to the term, involves the negotiation of individual presence within a transhistorical recurrence of lyric gestures, which are not necessarily translated into a stable phrasing to be found in a specific text and then reused.

19 Harold Bloom, *The Anxiety of Influence: A Theory of Poetry* (Oxford: Oxford University Press, 1973).

20 Jonathan Culler, *Theory of the Lyric* (Cambridge, MA: Harvard University Press, 2015), p. 187. Tied to actual subjects, the idea can already be

in its transhistorical dimension, as a less rigid form. It is not a text to be simply repeated, but rather a repertoire of gestures and rhetorical structures that, depending on the historical context of performance, may or may not come already arranged in verbal fragments. Different historical subjectivities can re-enact those gestures either in writing or in reading.[21] The verbal gesture performed in the poem is thus recognized as still viable. Indeed, lyric speech asks to be validated by its reader. For this reason, the lyric is not the expression of an individual's uniqueness, but rather the partial renunciation of enclosed particularity

found in Helen Vendler, *Poems, Poets, Poetry: An Introduction and Anthology* (Boston: Bedford/St. Martin's, 1997): '[A] lyric is meant to be spoken by its reader as if the reader were the one uttering the words. A lyric poem is a script for performance by its reader. It is, then, the most intimate of genres, constructing a twinship between writer and reader. And it is the most universal of genres, because it presumes that the reader resembles the writer enough to step into the writer's shoes and speak the lines the writer has written as though they were the reader's own' (pp. xl–xli). More than as an identification of two entities in accordance to a precise script, here the relationship is conceived as a more flexible performance of two processes following shared gestures that different subjectivities can perform without fully individuating themselves, therefore with no requirement of a complete assimilation. See Daniel Morris, *Lyric Encounters: Essays on American Poetry from Lazarus and Frost to Ortiz Cofer and Alexie* (London: Bloomsbury, 2013), pp. 1–2.

21 Paul Allen Miller, *Lyric Texts and Lyric Consciousness: The Birth of a Genre from Archaic Greece to Augustan Rome* (London: Routledge, 1994) locates the birth of the modern lyric subject — 'an individual and highly self-reflexive subjective consciousness' (p. 1) — in the writing culture developed in Augustan Rome and in the context of the production of authorial books of poetry. I would distinguish, as Dante implicitly does in the *Vita nova*, between the potential openness of the single poem, which offers a shareable subjective position of enunciation, and the projection of a subject or individual identity brought forth especially by the organized macrotext, which allows 'recursive modes of reading' (p. 2). The friction between the iterable single poem and the projection of an author, made possible by retrospective and multitemporal (self)-reading, is what Dante explores in the *Vita nova*.

in favour of an open mutuality.[22] In the act of *re-citing* a poem, the reader realizes a similarity of particularity (the situational experience) and generality (the shareable conditions). Although the act of speaking individuates the lyric subjectivity by marking its dissimilarity, it also places it within a potential transhistorical community. Instead of isolating a subject in an auto-referential self-sufficiency, the subjective position of lyric speaking may open to an acknowledgement of proximity through time.

22 See Jay M. Bernstein, 'Confession and Forgiveness: Hegel's Poetics of Action', in *Beyond Representation: Philosophy and Poetic Imagination*, ed. by Richard Eldridge (Cambridge: Cambridge University Press, 1996), pp. 34–65 (p. 48).

Revolution

Making a Break in History

ARIANNA SFORZINI

'Revolution' is a central concept in Western contemporary philosophy. Since Kant, and then Hegel and Marx, the term revolution has taken on a double meaning: (1) the embodiment of freedom in history, the sign of the openness of historical times, the ability to change, following the free practical human nature, and to progress towards the better; (2) the achievement of history itself — for example, a proletarian revolution in Marxist thought, which will accomplish the destruction of the old world and create the new communist era. Revolution is a capital turning point in the history of humanity, realizing human freedom and pushing it to its limits. When Kant, in his essay *The Conflict of the Faculties* (1798), reflects on the revolution that can be considered the beginning of the contemporary world — the French Revolution — he transforms it, in its pure revolutionary form, regardless of its historical context, results, or consequences, into a decisive moral and political sign. Is there any concrete moment in history that could indicate, reliably, that humanity as a whole advances towards improvement? Is there any historical event that proves progress in the moral world? For Kant, the French Revolution is this sign of progress, not as a specific political transformation but as a public event, filling the hearts of spectators with enthusiasm, sympathetic participation, and faith in the realization of justice. Revolution is the actualization of freedom, and the utopia of its achievement beyond all time and history.

The present contribution aims at analysing this double meaning of the revolution as an 'operational value in history'[1] through a particular group of articles Michel Foucault wrote and which have been more vigorously criticized than any other part of his œuvre: the reporting he did for *Il Corriere della Sera* during his two journeys to Iran in September and November 1978. In these articles, Foucault describes the revolts against the Shah's regime and suggests to read them against a certain understanding of the notion of revolution, through a fascinating and, at the same time, highly ambiguous concept: that of a 'political spirituality'.[2] I shall briefly analyse this notion, exploring its link to the Western notion of revolution. I shall then argue that, despite Foucault's rejection of this notion, revolution is still a very important concept to reactivate in order to think

1 Michel Foucault, *The Government of Self and Others. Lectures at the Collège de France, 1982–1983*, trans. by G. Burchell (London: Palgrave Macmillan, 2010), p. 20.

2 Michel Foucault, 'À quoi rêvent les Iraniens?' [1978], in *Dits et écrits*, ed. by Daniel Defert, François Ewald and Jacques Lagrange, 2 vols (Paris: Gallimard, 2001), II: *1976–1988*, text no. 245, p. 694: 'Quel sens, pour les hommes qui habitent [la terre d'Iran], à rechercher au prix même de leur vie cette chose dont nous avons, nous autres, oublié la possibilité depuis la Renaissance et les grandes crises du christianisme: une spiritualité politique.'

about the role and the possibility of political revolts and freedom today.

The Foucault Archive at the Bibliothèque nationale in Paris contains the complete set of documents Foucault gathered during and after his Iranian journeys. [3] I was most impressed by a journal of sorts Foucault kept while in Iran, full of historical, political, and personal notes about the country he was discovering. It shows a true journalistic spirit; the reader can feel Foucault's pleasure in discovering a country on the verge of a major political transformation and his desire to understand this historical turning point by analysing the economic, geopolitical, and cultural situation in Iran. He is not a philosopher looking at history from the superior standpoint of abstract reason, but a witness and a reporter giving voice to the historical fractures and forces he encounters on the ground.

Foucault is definitely fascinated by what could be called the 'negative character' of the Iranian revolt against Reza Pahlavi: it was a popular uprising, originated in a seemingly spontaneous way; there weren't, at the beginning, any main ideological directions, political parties, or institutions to guide it; and still, the revolt was massive, undivided, and capable of a major disruption of the political order. Foucault saw the rise of an entire unarmed people, united by the only aim of 'saying no to the Shah'. Before the return of Khomeini, the Shiite Islamic voices went along with the strong Marxist movement in Iran and other opposition forces. The religious state was a political utopia reconnecting with an idealized past, and Foucault couldn't imagine in 1978 that the revolt he was witnessing could result in an oppressive clerical regime. Most importantly, in

3 Michel Foucault Archives, Bibliothèque nationale de France, boîtes 50–50bis (NAF 28730).

his articles, he refuses to speak of an Iranian 'Revolution': this concept is for him ideologically charged, meaning a historical violent riot led and used by a political party, group, or class. One can say that Khomeini transformed the Iranian revolt into a revolution, but what Foucault first saw was a '*soulèvement*': the simple and negative opening of the possibility of a transformation in history; a disruption of the concrete political situation making room for something new to arise.

> Revolution organizes itself according to a temporal economy: conditions, promises, necessities; it resides thus in history, makes its bed in it, and ultimately lies in it. The uprising [le *soulèvement*], breaking the order of time, raises men upright against their land and their humanity.[4]

Did Foucault underestimate the power of the Islamic clergy? Definitely. But was Khomeini's regime really the only possible outcome of the revolt against the Shah? Yet more importantly, even after the religious and despotic turn in Iran, Foucault claimed the relevance of a notion he first used in his Iranian reportage: that of a 'political spirituality'. It is clearly an ambiguous expression, one which resulted at the end of the 1970s in a massive critique of the French philosopher, accusing him to have indirectly legitimated the Khomeinist regime. Actually, Foucault was far from imagining the theocratic outcome of the Iranian revolt. What he did see, however, was the massive

4 'La révolution s'organise selon toute une économie intérieure au temps: des conditions, des promesses, des nécessités; elle loge donc dans l'histoire, y fait son lit et finalement s'y couche. Le soulèvement, coupant le temps, dresse les hommes à la verticale de leur terre et de leur humanité.' ('Vivre autrement le temps' [1979], in *Dits et écrits*, II: text no. 267, pp. 788–90 (p. 790) [my translation]).

potential of a revolt rooted in a religious and existential dimension.

The importance of Foucault's articles lies in the insights they provide into the essential role Islam and its 'political spirituality' — Islam as a 'political force'[5] — was and arguably is to play in the contemporary geopolitical world. Foucault sees in the Iranian revolts and in the revolutionary energy unleashed by their mobilization of Islamic religion a new form of opposition to state power, that is to say: to a modern Western political order, its army, its police, its embassies. The Iranian revolt is, in Foucault's eyes, a 'counter-behaviour' to the governmentality of the modern state. As such, it can serve as a privileged platform for political observation and experimentation. The Western-style 'modernization' coveted by the Shah and by United States policy towards Iran is actually an attempt to reproduce Eurocentric models of state organization. And the revolts against these attempts are for Foucault 'perhaps the first great insurrection against global systems, the form of revolt that is the most modern and the most insane'.[6] In Iran, religion proves to be a force that is able to oppose the existential and political constraints of the very modern state whose history Foucault had so tirelessly reconstructed in order to find news ways to criticize it.

Foucault is aware that Islam risks becoming 'a gigantic powder-keg' on a global scale.[7] His statements are clearly relevant today, in light of what has since happened in the

5 Michel Foucault, 'Foucault's Response to Atoussa H.' [1978], trans. by Karen de Bruin and Kevin B. Anderson, in Janet Afary and Kevin B. Anderson, *Foucault and the Iranian Revolution: Gender and the Seductions of Islamism* (Chicago: University of Chicago Press, 2005), p. 210.

6 Michel Foucault, 'The Mythical Leader of the Iranian Revolt' [1978], trans. by Karen de Bruin and Kevin B. Anderson, in Afary and Anderson, *Foucault and the Iranian Revolution*, pp. 220–23 (p. 222).

7 Michel Foucault, 'A Powder Keg Called Islam' [1979], trans. by Karen

Middle East and in Europe: the rise of religious radicalism, the increasing numbers of migrants fleeing conflicts in Islamic countries, the West's difficulties in intervening and imposing its control and its security strategies. Foucault interrogates the field of ethical-political subjectivation for a Europe (a European way of conceiving of the state) that is in decline and a West which is globalizing the world, yet finds itself called into question by this very process of globalization. Through his reflections on the particular case of Iran, he raises the general question: beyond the European identity crisis, how, and by means of what poles and relations, do we create political subjectivities?

Paradoxically enough, Foucault deploys a massive set of knowledge about Iranian history and Islamic religion in order to develop a strictly Eurocentric reflection on revolt and revolution. Foucault said the Iranian revolt was not, at its beginning, a revolution, as it was not dominated by an ideology. And yet, it was a concrete example of what revolution has meant in Western thought since Kant and the French Revolution: the opening of new possibilities in time and history, demanding a form of philosophical discourse which is no longer the ahistorical investigation of the universal conditions of human thought but the response to actual political needs. Foucault's various analyses of Kant's 1784 essay 'An Answer to the Question: What is Enlightenment' prove this point: revolution has been, for the contemporary Western world, the actual evidence that history is an open process, through which it has to rethink and test its forms of discourse, thought, and existence. Could Iran and its 'revolt/revolution' play the same

---

de Bruin and Kevin B. Anderson, in Afary and Anderson, *Foucault and the Iranian Revolution*, pp. 239–41 (p. 241).

role of critique for 1970s and 1980s Europe, and maybe for today's world?

Foucault's controversial concept of 'political spirituality' must not be thought as a sort of apologetic of a political power built on religion. Rather, it conveys the important idea that a true political movement cannot exist unless it is built on an existential transformation — that is the sense of the notion of 'spirituality' used by Foucault later, in the 1980s, to indicate the exercises of the self. In all likelihood, Foucault stresses the fact that religion is (and has been in Western history) a massive political force also strategically, against the French doctrine of laicism as a sort of 'anaesthetization' of the political sphere. The real question Foucault poses to the present moment would then be: are political spirituality and revolution possible outside ideological dogmas? Which political energy can be deployed today that is rooted in existential practices and strong enough to be the motor of historical change?

References

BIBLIOGRAPHY

Afary, Janet, and Kevin B. Anderson, *Foucault and the Iranian Revolution: Gender and the Seductions of Islamism* (Chicago: University of Chicago Press, 2005)

Agacinski, Sylviane, 'Anachronisms of Art: Style and Medium', in *Time Passing: Modernity and Nostalgia,* trans. by Jody Gladding (New York: Columbia University Press, 2003), pp. 105–36

Agamben, Giorgio, *The Church and the Kingdom,* trans. by Leland de la Durantaye (Chicago: The University of Chicago Press, 2012)

—— 'The End of the Poem', in *The End of the Poem: Studies in Poetics,* trans. by Daniel Heller-Roazen (Stanford: Stanford University Press, 1999)

—— *The Kingdom and the Glory: For a Theological Genealogy of Economy and Government. Homo Sacer II, 4,* trans. by Lorenzo Chiesa (Stanford: Stanford University Press, 2007)

—— 'Leviathan's Riddle', in *Leviathans Rätsel,* trans. by Paul Silas Peterson (Tübingen: Mohr Siebeck, 2013)

—— *The Mystery of Evil: Benedict XVI and the End of Days,* trans. by Adam Kotsko (Stanford: Stanford University Press, 2017)

—— 'Notes on Gesture', in *Infancy and History: The Destruction of Experience,* trans. by Liz Heron (London: Verso, 1993), pp. 133–40

—— *Stasis: Civil War as a Political Paradigm. Homo Sacer II, 2,* trans. by Nicholas Heron (Stanford: Stanford University Press, 2015)

—— *The Time That Remains: A Commentary on the Letter to the Romans,* trans. by Patricia Dailey (Stanford: Stanford University Press, 2005)

Agnew, Vanessa, 'History's Affective Turn: Historical Reenactment and Its Work in the Present',

Rethinking History, 11.3 (2007), pp. 299–312 <https://doi.org/10.1080/13642520701353108>

American Psychiatric Association, ed., *Diagnostic and Statistical Manual of Mental Disorders, Fifth Edition*, DSM-5 (Washington, DC: American Psychiatric Publishing, 2013)

Anker, Elizabeth S., and Rita Felski, 'Introduction', in *Critique and Postcritique*, ed. by Anker and Felski (Durham, NC: Duke University Press, 2017), pp. 1–28

Attridge, Derek, *The Work of Literature* (Oxford: Oxford University Press, 2015)

Augustine, *Confessions*, ed. and trans. by Carolyn J.-B. Hammond, 2 vols (Cambridge, MA: Harvard University Press, 2014–16)

Austin, John L., *How to Do Things with Words* (Cambridge, MA: Harvard University Press, 1975)

Bach, Johann Sebastian, Staatsbibliothek zu Berlin, MS Mus. ms. autogr. Bach P200/1, fascicle 3, p. 39, <https://www.bach-digital.de/rsc/viewer/BachDigitalSource_derivate_00062812/db_bachp0200-1_page039.jpg> [accessed 8 December 2018]

Bakhtin, Mikhail, 'Discourse in the Novel', in *The Dialogic Imagination: Four Essays*, ed. by Michael Holquist, trans. by Michael Holquist and Caryl Emerson (Austin: University of Texas Press, 1981), pp. 259–422

Baldacci, Cristina, 'Re-enactment e altre storie. Dall'archivio alla contro-narrazione per immagini nell'arte contemporanea', *La rivista di Engramma*, 150 (2017), pp. 41–48 <http://www.engramma.it/eOS/index.php?id_articolo=3215> [accessed 18 December 2018]

Baldacci, Cristina, and Clio Nicastro, 'Il Bilderatlas Mnemosyne ri-visitato: una mostra e un convegno a Karlsruhe', *La rivista di Engramma*, 142 (2017) <http://www.engramma.it/eOS/index.php?id_articolo=3086> [accessed 18 December 2018]

Barański, Zygmunt G., 'Dante Alighieri: Experimentation and (Self-)Exegesis', in *The Cambridge History of Literary Criticism*, ed. by H. B. Nisbet and Claude Rawson, 9 vols (Cambridge: Cambridge University Press, 1989–), II: *The Middle Ages*, ed. by Alastair Minnis and Ian Johnson (2005), pp. 561–82

Barolini, Teodolinda, '"Cominciandomi dal principio infino a la fine" (*V.N.*, XXIII, 15): Forging Anti-Narrative in the "Vita Nuova"', in *La gloriosa donna de la mente: A Commentary on the* Vita Nuova, ed. by Vincent Moleta (Florence: Olschki, 1994)

Belting, Hans, *An Anthropology of Images: Picture, Medium, Body*, trans. by Thomas Dunlap (Princeton: Princeton University Press, 2011)

Bénichou, Anne, ed., *Recréer/Scripter. Mémoires et transmissions des œuvres performatives et chorégraphiques contemporaines* (Dijon: Presses du réel, 2015)

Benjamin, Walter, *Gesammelte Schriften*, ed. by Rolf Tiedemann and Hermann Schweppenhäuser, 7 vols (Frankfurt a.M.: Suhrkamp, 1972–91)

—— 'Einbahnstraße', in *GS* IV: *Kleine Prosa, Baudelaire-Übertragungen* (1972), pp. 83–148

—— 'Karl Kraus', in *GS* II: *Aufsätze, Essays, Vorträge* (1977), pp. 335–67

—— '"El mayor monstruo, los celos" von Calderón und "Herodes und Mariamne" von Hebbel. Bemerkungen zum Problem des historischen Dramas', in *GS* II: *Aufsätze, Essays, Vorträge* (1977), pp. 246–76

—— *Das Passagen-Werk*, in *GS* V: *Das Passagen-Werk* (1982)

—— 'Schemata zu "Karl Kraus" <1>', in *GS* II: *Aufsätze, Essays, Vorträge* (1977), pp. 1091–94

—— 'Zentralpark', in *GS* I: *Abhandlungen* (1974), pp. 655–90

Berlant, Lauren, 'Slow Death (Obesity, Sovereignty, Lateral Agency)', in *Cruel Optimism*, (Durham, NC: Duke University Press, 2011), pp. 95–119

Bernstein, Jay M., 'Confession and Forgiveness: Hegel's Poetics of Action', in *Beyond Representation: Philosophy and Poetic Imagination*, ed. by Richard Eldridge (Cambridge: Cambridge University Press, 1996), pp. 34–65

Bloom, Harold, *The Anxiety of Influence: A Theory of Poetry* (Oxford: Oxford University Press, 1973)

Bolter, Jay D., and Richard A. Grusin, *Remediation: Understanding New Media* (Cambridge, MA: MIT Press, 1999)

Bray, Abigail, 'The Anorexic Body: Reading Disorders', *Cultural Studies*, 10.3 (1996) <https://doi.org/10.1080/09502389600490251>

Budick, Sanford, and Wolfgang Iser, eds, *Languages of the Unsay-*

able: The Play of Negativity in Literature and Literary Theory (New York: Columbia University Press, 1989)

Butler, Judith, *Frames of War: When is Life Grievable?* (London: Verso, 2009)

—— *Precarious Life: The Powers of Mourning and Violence* (London: Verso, 2004)

Cacciari, Massimo, *The Withholding Power: An Essay on Political Theology*, trans. by Edi Pucci (London: Bloomsbury, 2018)

Carlson, Marvin, 'Living History, Re-enactment', in *Performance Studies: Key Words, Concepts and Theories*, ed. by Bryan Reynolds (London: Palgrave, 2014), pp. 84–90

Casetti, Francesco, and Antonio Somaini, 'The Conflict Between High Definition and Low Definition in Contemporary Cinema', *Convergence*, 19.4 (2013), pp. 415–22 <https://doi.org/10.1177/1354856513494174>

Celant, Germano, ed., *When Attitudes Become Form: Bern 1969/Venice 2013* (Milan: Fondazione Prada, 2013)

Centanni, Monica, 'Editoriale: Engramma da 0 a 100', *Engramma*, 100 (2012) <http://www.engramma.it/eOS/index.php?id_articolo=1161> [accessed 18 December 2018]

Chabert, Garance, and Aurélien Mole, eds, *Les Artistes iconographes/Artists as Iconographers* (Paris: Empire Books, 2018)

Collingwood, Robin G., *The Idea of History* (Oxford: Clarendon Press, 1946)

Comay, Rebecca, 'Benjamin's Endgame', in *Walter Benjamin's Philosophy*, ed. by Andrew Benjamin and Peter Osborne (London: Routledge, 1993)

Coyle, Robert, *'RE': God's Favorite Prefix* (Montgomery, AL: E-BookTime, 2013)

Culler, Jonathan, *Theory of the Lyric* (Cambridge, MA: Harvard University Press, 2015)

Dante, *Rime giovanili e della* Vita nuova, ed. by Teodolinda Barolini, notes by Manuele Gragnolati (Milano: Rizzoli Bur, 2009)

—— *Vita nova*, ed. by Guglielmo Gorni (Turin: Einaudi, 1996); in English as *Dante's* Vita Nuova. *New Edition: A Translation and an Essay*, ed. and trans. by Mark Musa (Bloomington: Indiana University Press, 1973)

Deleuze, Gilles, *Difference and Repetition* [1968], trans. by Paul R. Patton (New York: Columbia University Press, 1994)

—— *The Logic of Sense* [1969], trans. by Mark Lester and Charles Stivale (New York: Columbia University Press, 1990)

—— *Proust et les Signes* (Paris: PUF, 1964), in English as *Proust and Signs*, trans. by Richard Howard (London: Continuum, 2008)

Derrida, Jacques, 'Letter to a Japanese Friend', trans. by David Wood and Andrew Benjamin, in *Derrida, Psyché: Inventions of the Other II*, ed. by Peggy Kamuf and Elizabeth Rottenberg (Stanford: Stanford University Press, 2008), pp. 1–6

Doubrovsky, Serge, *La Place de la madeleine. Ecriture et fantasme chez Proust* (Grenoble: ELLUG, 2000)

Dray, William H., *History as Re-enactment: R. G. Collingwood's Idea of History* (Oxford: Oxford University Press, 1995)

Eliot, T. S., 'The Three Voices of Poetry', in *On Poetry and Poets* (London: Faber and Faber, 1957), pp. 89–102

Elman, Julie Passanante, *Chronic Youth: Disability, Sexuality, and U.S. Media Cultures of Rehabilitation* (New York: New York University Press, 2014)

Ernst, Wolfgang, *The Delayed Present: Media-Induced Tempor(e)alities & Techno-Traumatic Irritations of 'the Contemporary'* (Berlin: Sternberg Press, 2017)

Esposito, Roberto, *Immunitas: The Protection and Negation of Life*, trans. by Zakiya Hanafi (Cambridge: Polity, 2011)

—— *Two: The Machine of Political Theology and the Place of Thought*, trans. by Zakiya Hanafi (New York: Fordham University Press, 2015)

Federici, Silvia, *The Caliban and the Witch: Woman, the Body and Primitive Accumulation* (New York: Autonomedia, 2004)

Felski, Rita, *The Limits of Critique* (Chicago: University of Chicago Press, 2015)

—— 'Response', in 'On Rita Felski's *The Limits of Critique*', *PMLA*, 132.2 (March 2017), pp. 384–91

Fink, Robert, *Repeating Ourselves: American Minimal Music as Cultural Practice* (Berkeley: University of California Press, 2005)

Foucault, Michel, *Dits et écrits*, ed. by Daniel Defert, François Ewald, and Jacques Lagrange, 2 vols (Paris: Gallimard, 2001)

—— 'À quoi rêvent les Iraniens?', in *Dits et écrits*, II: 1976–1988, text no. 245, pp. 688–94 (first publ. in *Nouvel Observateur*, 727 [16 October 1978], pp. 48–49)

—— 'Ariane s'est pendue', in *Dits et écrits*, I: *1954–1975*, text no. 64, pp. 795–799 (first publ. in *Nouvel Observateur*, 229 [31 March 1969], pp. 36–37)

—— Boîte 53, Archives Foucault, Bibliothèque nationale de France (NAF 28730)

—— Boîtes 50–50bis, Archives Foucault, Bibliothèque nationale de France (NAF 28730)

—— 'Ceci n'est pas une pipe', in *Dits et écrits*, I: *1954–1975*, text no. 53, pp. 663–78 (first publ. in *Les Cahiers du chemin*, 2 [15 January 1968], pp. 79–105), in English as *This Is Not a Pipe*, trans. by James Harkness (Berkeley: University of California Press, 1983)

—— *The Government of Self and Others. Lectures at the Collège de France, 1982–1983*, trans. by Graham Burchell (London: Palgrave Macmillan, 2010)

—— 'Il mitico capo della rivolta dell'Iran (Le chef mythique de la révolte de l'Iran)', in *Dits et écrits*, II: *1976–1988*, text no. 253, pp. 713–16 (first publ. in *Corriere della sera*, 103.279 [26 November 1978], pp. 1–2), in English as 'The Mythical Leader of the Iranian Revolt', trans. by Karen de Bruin and Kevin B. Anderson, in Afary and Anderson, *Foucault and the Iranian Revolution*, pp. 220–23

—— 'Una polveriera chiamata islam (Une poudriere appelée islam)', in *Dits et écrits*, II: *1976–1988*, text no. 261, pp. 759–61 (first publ. in *Corriere della sera*, 104.36 [13 February 1979], p. 1), in English as 'A Powder Keg Called Islam', trans. by Karen de Bruin and Kevin B. Anderson, in Afary and Anderson, *Foucault and the Iranian Revolution*, pp. 239–41

—— 'Réponse de Michel Foucault à une lectrice iranienne', in *Dits et écrits*, II: *1976–1988*, text no. 251, p. 708 (first publ. in *Nouvel Observateur*, 731 [13 November 1978], p. 26), in English as 'Foucault's Response to Atoussa H.', trans. by Karen de Bruin and Kevin B. Anderson, in Afary and Anderson, *Foucault and the Iranian Revolution*, p. 210

—— 'Theatrum philosophicum', in *Dits et écrits*, I: *1954–1975*, text no. 80 (first publ. in *Critique*, 282 [November 1970], pp. 885–908), in English as 'Theatrum philosophicum', trans. by Donald F. Brouchard and Sherry Simon, in *Essential Works of Foucault, 1954–1984*, ed. by Paul Rabinow, 3 vols (New York: New Press, 1998–2001), II: *Aesthetics, Method, and Epistemology*, ed. by James D. Faubion (1998), pp. 343–68

—— 'Vivre autrement le temps', in *Dits et écrits*, II: *1976–1988*, text no. 267, pp. 788–90 (first publ. in *Nouvel Observateur*, 755 [30 April 1979], p. 88)

Franke, William, *A Philosophy of the Unsayable* (Notre Dame, IN: University of Notre Dame Press, 2014)

—— *Poetry and Apocalypse: Theological Disclosures of Poetic Language* (Stanford: Stanford University Press, 2009)

Freeman, Elizabeth, *Time Binds: Queer Temporalities, Queer Histories* (Durham, NC: Duke University Press, 2010)

Freeman, Hadley, 'To the Bone Confirms There Are (Almost) No Good Movies about Anorexia', *Guardian*, 12 July 2017 <https://www.theguardian.com/film/2017/jul/12/to-the-bone-confirms-there-are-almost-no-good-movies-about-anorexia> [accessed 21 September 2018]

Freud, Sigmund, *Gesammelte Werke*, 17 vols (London: Imago, 1940–52)

—— *The Standard Edition of the Complete Psychological Works of Sigmund Freud*, ed. and trans. by James Strachey, 24 vols (London: Hogarth, 1953–74)

—— *Beyond the Pleasure Principle*, in *The Standard Edition*, XVIII: *Beyond the Pleasure Principle, Group Psychology and Other Works (1920–22)* (1955), pp. 1–64

—— 'Erinnern, Wiederholen und Durcharbeiten', in *Gesammelte Werke*, X: *Werke aus den Jahren 1913–1917* (1946), pp. 125–36; in English as 'Remembering, Repeating and Working-Through (Further Recommendations on the Technique of Psycho-Analysis II) (1914)', in *The Standard Edition*, XII: *The Case of Schreber, Papers on Technique and Other Works* (1958), pp. 145–56

—— *The Interpretation of Dreams*, in *The Standard Edition*, IV–V (1953)

Frye, Northrop, *The Anatomy of Criticism: Four Essays* (Princeton: Princeton University Press, 1957)

Gaillard, Julie, 'The Task of Thinking (in) The Postmodern Space of "The Zone"', in *Traversals of Affect*, ed. by J. Gaillard, C. Nouvet, and M. Stoholski, pp. 229–46

Gaillard, Julie, Claire Nouvet, and Mark Stoholski, eds, *Traversals of Affect: On Jean-François Lyotard* (London: Bloomsbury, 2016)

Gay, Roxane, *Hunger* (New York: HarperCollins, 2017)

Genette, Gérard, *The Architext: An Introduction*, trans. by Jane E. Lewin (Berkeley: University of California Press, 1992)

Gioni, Massimiliano, and Andrea Pinotti, 'Images of Images: The Survival and Repetition of Forms. A Conversation between Massimiliano Gioni and Andrea Pinotti', in *To Write an Image*, ed. by Vincenzo de Bellis (Milan: Mousse Publishing, 2015), pp. 17–27

Giusti, Francesco, *Il desiderio della lirica. Poesia, creazione, conoscenza* (Rome: Carocci Editore, 2016)

—— 'The Lyric in Theory. A Conversation with Jonathan Culler', *Los Angeles Review of Books*, 27 May 2017

Gombrich, Ernst H., *Aby Warburg: An Intellectual Biography* (London: Warburg Institute, 1970)

Gragnolati, Manuele, and Francesca Southerden, 'Dalla perdita al possesso. Forme di temporalità non lineare nelle epifanie liriche di Cavalcanti, Dante e Petrarca', *Chroniques italiennes*, séries web 32 (1/2017), pp. 136–54 <http://www.univ-paris3.fr/medias/fichier/gragnolati-southerden_1501152291404.pdf> [accessed 20 December 2018]

Gragnolati, Manuele, and Christoph F. E. Holzhey, eds, *De/Constituting Wholes: Towards Partiality Without Parts* (Vienna: Turia + Kant, 2017)

Green, Dennis H., *The Beginnings of Medieval Romance: Fact and Fiction, 1150–1220* (Cambridge: Cambridge University Press, 2002)

Grossheutschi, Felix, *Carl Schmitt und die Lehre vom Katechon* (Berlin: Duncker & Humblot, 1996)

Groys, Boris, 'Art in the Age of Biopolitics: From Artwork to Art Documentation', in *Art Power* (Cambridge, MA: MIT Press, 2008), pp. 53–65

—— 'Art Topology: The Reproduction of Aura', in *When Attitudes Become Form*, ed. by G. Celant, pp. 451–56

Hamann, Johann Georg, *Schriften*, ed. Friedrich Roth, 7 vols (Berlin: Riemer, 1821–25)

Hansen, Gitte Marianne, *Femininity, Self-Harm and Eating Dis-*

orders in Japan. Navigating Contradiction in Narrative and Visual Culture (London: Routledge, 2016)

Harrison, Robert Pogue, *The Body of Beatrice* (Baltimore: Johns Hopkins University Press, 1988)

Hartman, Saidiya, 'The Terrible Beauty of the Slum' (2017) <https://brickmag.com/the-terrible-beauty-of-the-slum/> [accessed 20 December 2018]

Holmes, Su, '(Un)twisted: Talking Back to Media Representations of Eating Disorders', *Journal of Gender Studies*, 27.3 (May 2016), pp. 1–16 <https://doi.org/10.1080/09589236.2016.1181539>

Holy Bible: New International Version (Colorado Springs: Biblica, 1984)

Holzhey, Christoph F. E., ed., *Multistable Figures: On the Critical Potentials of Ir/Reversible Aspect-Seeing* (Vienna: Turia + Kant, 2014)

—— ed., *Tension/Spannung* (Vienna: Turia + Kant, 2010) <https://doi.org/10.25620/ci-01>

Holzhey, Helmut, 'Neukantianismus', in *Historisches Wörterbuch der Philosophie*, ed. by Joachim Ritter, Karlfried Gründer, and Gottfried Gabriel, 13 vols (Basel: Schwabe, 1971–2007), VI (1984), pp. 747–54

Jackson, Virginia, and Yopie Prins, eds, *The Lyric Theory Reader. A Critical Anthology* (Baltimore: Johns Hopkins University Press, 2014)

Jameson, Fredric, 'Foreword: A Monument to Radical Instants', in Weiss, *The Aesthetics of Resistance*, pp. vii–xlix

Jarrety, Michel, 'The Poetics of Practice and Theory', in *Reading Paul Valéry: Universe in Mind*, ed. by Paul Gifford and Brian Stimpson (Cambridge: Cambridge University Press, 1998)

Jean Starobinski, *Action and Reaction: The Life and Adventures of a Couple*, trans. by Sophie Hawkes (New York: Zone Books, 2003)

Johnson, Merri Lisa, and Robert McRuer, 'Cripistemologies: Introduction', *Journal of Literary & Cultural Disability Studies*, 8.2 (2014), pp. 127–47 <https://doi.org/10.3828/jlcds.2014.21>

Johnson, W. R., *The Idea of Lyric: Lyric Modes in Ancient and Modern Poetry* (Berkeley: University of California Press, 1982)

Johnson, W. Ralph, *The Idea of Lyric: Lyric Modes in Ancient and Modern Poetry* (Berkeley: University of California Press, 1982)

Jones, Amelia, '"The Artist Is Present": Artistic Re-enactments and the Impossibility of Presence', *TDR: The Drama Review*, 55.1 (2011), pp. 16–45 <https://doi.org/10.1162/DRAM_a_00046>

—— 'The Now and the Has Been: Paradoxes of Live Art in History', in *Perform, Repeat, Record: Live Art in History* , ed. by Amelia Jones and Adrian Heathfield (Bristol: Intellect, 2012)

Kant, Immanuel, *An Answer to the Question: What Is Enlightenment*, ed. and trans. by Mary J. Gregor (Cambridge: Cambridge University Press, 1996), pp. 11–22

—— *The Conflict of the Faculties*, trans. by Mary J. Gregor and Robert Anchor, in *Religion and Rational Theology*, ed. by Allen W. Wood and George di Giovanni (Cambridge: Cambridge University Press, 1996), pp. 233–327

Kierkegaard, Søren, *Søren Kierkegaards Skrifter elektronisk version 1.8.1*, ed. by Karsten Kynde (Copenhagen: Søren Kierkegaard Forskningscenteret, 2014), 'Journaler og papirer', DD:28 <http://www.sks.dk/DD/txt.xml> [accessed 16 December 2018]

King, Elisabeth, 'Are Movies about Eating Disorders Fundamentally Uncinematic?', *Pacific Standard*, 14 July 2017 <https://psmag.com/social-justice/how-to-make-a-movie-about-a-lonely-terrible-experience> [accessed 21 September 2018]

Köbler, Gerhard, *Lateinisches Abkunfts- und Wirkungswörterbuch*, 2nd edn (2009) <http://www.koeblergerhard.de/Latein/LateinischesWB.pdf> [accessed 20 December 2018]

Konstantinovsky, Michelle, 'Eating Disorders Do Not Discriminate: Puncturing the Dangerous Myth That Only White Women Get Eating Disorders', *Slate*, 20 March 2014 <http://www.slate.com/articles/double_x/doublex/2014/03/eating_disorders_and_women_of_color_anorexia_and_bulimia_are_not_just_white.html> [accessed 21 September 2018]

Kristeva, Julia, 'Entretien: La Transsubstanciation de Proust: une suspension du refoulement', in *Marcel Proust, visiteur des psychanalystes*, ed. by Andrée Bauduin and Françoise Coblenc (Paris: PUF, 2003), pp. 63–95

—— *Le Temps sensible. Proust et l'expérience littéraire* (Paris: Gallimard, 2000)

—— 'Word, Dialogue, and Novel', in *Desire in Language: A Semiotic Approach to Literature and Art*, ed. by Leon S. Roudiez, trans. by Thomas Gora, Alice Jardine, and Leon S. Roudiez (New York: Columbia University Press, 1980), pp. 64–91

Law, Vivien, 'The Middle Ages', in *Morphologie / Morphology: Ein internationales Handbuch zur Flexion und Wortbildung / An International Handbook on Inflection and Word-Formation*, ed. by Geert Booij, Christian Lehmann, and Joachim Mugdan (Berlin: DeGruyter, 2000), pp. 76–90

Lepecki, André, 'The Body as Archive: Will to Re-enact and the Afterlives of Dances', *Dance Research Journal*, 42.2 (2010), pp. 28–48 <https://doi.org/10.1017/S0149767700001029>

Levine, Emily J., *Hamburg, Dreamland of Humanists: Warburg, Cassirer, Panofsky, and the Hamburg School* (Chicago: University of Chicago Press, 2013)

Lindner, Burkhardt, and Christian Rogowski, 'Between Pergamon and Plötzensee: Another Way of Depicting the Course of Events an Interview with Peter Weiss', *New German Critique*, 30 (Autumn 1983), pp. 107–26

Linebaugh, Peter, and Marcus Rediker, *The Many-Headed Hydra: Sailors, Slaves, Commoners, and the Hidden History of the Revolutionary Atlantic* (Boston: Beacon, 2013)

Lissoni, Andrea, ed., *Philippe Parreno: H{n)ypn(y}osis/Hypothesis* (Milan: Mousse Publishing, 2017)

Love, Heather, *Feeling Backward: Loss and the Politics of Queer History* (Cambridge, MA: Harvard University Press, 2007)

—— 'Truth and Consequences: On Paranoid Reading and Reparative Reading', *Criticism*, 52.2 (Spring 2010), pp. 235-41

Lütticken, Sven, *History in Motion: Time in the Age of the Moving Image* (Berlin: Sternberg Press, 2013)

Lyotard, Jean-François, *Heidegger and 'the jews'*, transl. by Andreas Michel and Mark S. Robert (Minneapolis: University of Minnesota Press, 1990)

—— *L'Inhumain. Causeries sur le temps* (Paris: Klincksiesck, 2014), in English as *The Inhuman: Reflections on Time,* transl. by Geoffrey Bennington and Rachel Bowlby (Cambridge: Polity, 1991)

—— '*Domus* et la mégapole', in *L'Inhumain*, pp. 181–92, in English as '*Domus* and the Megalopolis', in *The Inhuman*, pp. 191–204

—— 'La Peinture, anamnèse du visible', in *Misère de la philosophie* (Paris: Galilée, 2000), pp. 97–115

Malson, Helen, and Maree Burns, *Critical Feminist Approaches to Eating Dis/Orders* (London: Routledge, 2009)

Mandel, Ernest, 'Trotsky in Exile' [programme notes from the 1971 London production] <https://www.marxists.org/archive/mandel/1971/xx/exile.htm> [accessed 15 December 2018]

McEwan, Dorothea, 'A Tale of One Institute and Two Cities: The Warburg Institute', *Yearbook of the Research Centre for German and Austrian Exile Studies*, 1 (1999): *German-Speaking Exiles in Great Britain*, ed. by Ian Wallace, pp. 25–42

McGee, Micki, *Self Help, Inc.: Makeover Culture in American Life* (Oxford: Oxford University Press, 2005)

McRuer, Robert, *Crip Theory: Cultural Signs of Queerness and Disability* (New York: New York University Press, 2006)

Mecchia, Giuseppina, 'Proustiens, encore un effort… ! La déconstruction de l'inceste maternel dans *À la recherche du temps perdu*', *French Forum*, 31.3 (Fall 2006), pp. 77–96 <https://doi.org/10.1353/frf.2007.0027>

Meinhardt, Helmut, 'Neuplatonismus', in *Historisches Wörterbuch der Philosophie*, VI (1984), pp. 754–56

Menge, Hermann, *Langenscheidts Großwörterbuch Latein*, 2 vols (Berlin: Langenscheidt, 2001), II: *Lateinisch-deutsch, unter Berücksichtigung der Etymologie*

Merriam-Webster Online Dictionary, 'Reenact' <https://www.merriam-webster.com/dictionary/reenact> [accessed 18 December 2018]

Mertens, Wim, *American Minimal Music*, trans. by J. Hautekiet (New York: Broude, 1983)

Metzger, Paul, *Katechon: II Thess 2, 1–12 im Horizont apokalyptischen Denkens* (Berlin: De Gruyter, 2005)

Meyer, Robert, Conrad Schetter, and Janosh Prinz, 'Spatial Contestation? The Theological Foundations of Carl Schmitt's

Spatial Thought', *Geoforum*, 43 (2012), pp. 687–96 <https://doi.org/10.1016/j.geoforum.2011.06.004>

Mill, John Stuart, 'What is Poetry?', *The Monthly Repository*, n.s., 7 (1833), pp. 60–70

Miller, Paul Allen, *Lyric Texts and Lyric Consciousness: The Birth of a Genre from Archaic Greece to Augustan Rome* (London: Routledge, 1994)

Morin, Edgar, 'RE: From Prefix to Paradigm', *World Futures*, 61 (2005), pp. 254–67

Morris, Daniel, *Lyric Encounters: Essays on American Poetry from Lazarus and Frost to Ortiz Cofer and Alexie* (London: Bloomsbury, 2013)

Nagel, Alexander, and Christopher S. Wood, *Anachronic Renaissance* (New York: Zone Books, 2010)

Nouvet, Claire, 'For "Emma"', in *Traversals of Affect*, ed. by J. Gaillard, C. Nouvet, and M. Stoholski, pp. 37–54

—— 'The Inarticulate Affect: Lyotard and Psychoanalytic Testimony', in *Minima Memoria: In the Wake of Jean-François Lyotard*, ed. by Claire Nouvet, Kent Still, and Zrinka Stahuljak (Stanford: Stanford University Press, 2007), pp. 106–22

Novum Testamentum Graece, ed. by Eberhard Nestle, Barbara Aland, and Kurt Aland (Stuttgart: Deutsche Bibelgesellschaft, 2012)

OED Online (Oxford: Oxford University Press, 2000–) <http://www.oed.com> [accessed 3 January 2018]

Olson, Greta, *Reading Eating Disorders: Writings on Bulimia and Anorexia as Confessions of American Culture* (Frankfurt a.M.: Peter Lang, 2003)

Olson, Marisa, 'Lost Not Found: The Circulation of Images in Digital Visual Culture', in *Words Without Pictures*, ed. by Alex Klein (Los Angeles: LACMA, 2009), pp. 274–84

—— 'Postinternet: Art After the Internet', *Foam Magazine*, 29 (2011), pp. 59–63

Osborne, Peter, 'Archive as Afterlife and Life of Art', in *WERE IT AS IF: Beyond an Institution that Is*, ed. by Bik van der Pol and Defne Ayas (Rotterdam: Witte de With Center for Contemporary Art, 2017), pp. 49–53

Paglen, Trevor, 'Invisible Images (Your Pictures Are Looking at You)', *The New Inquiry*, 8 December 2016 <https://thenewinquiry.com/invisible-images-your-

pictures-are-looking-at-you/> [accessed 18 December 2018]

—— 'Operational Images', *e-flux journal*, 59 (2014) <https://www.e-flux.com/journal/59/61130/operational-images/> [accessed 18 December 2018]

Parr, Adrian, 'Deterritorialization/Reterritorialization' and 'Repetition', in *The Deleuze Dictionary*, revised edn, ed. by Parr (Edinburgh: Edinburgh University Press, 2010), pp. 69–72 and 225–26

Pinotti, Andrea, *Memorie del neutro. Morfologia dell'immagine in Aby Warburg* (Milan: Mimesis, 2001)

—— 'Optic Distance, Haptic Immersion', in *The Encyclopedic Palace*, ed. by Massimiliano Gioni and Natalie Bell (Venice: La Biennale di Venezia–Marsilio, 2013), pp. 193–94

Preciado, Paul B., 'Lives and Works of Lorenza Böttner', *South as a State of Mind*, 9 [documenta 14 #4] ([2017]) <https://www.documenta14.de/en/south/25298_lives_and_works_of_lorenza_boettner> [accessed 10 December 2018]

Proust, Marcel, *À la recherche du temps perdu*, 7 vols, ed. by Jean-Yves Tadié and others (Paris: Gallimard, 1988–90), in English as *In Search of Lost Time*, 6 vols, trans. by C. K. Scott Moncrieff and Terence Kilmartin, rev. by D. J. Enright (New York: Modern Library, 1992)

Prozorov, Sergei, 'The Katechon in the Age of Biopolitical Nihilism', *Continental Philosophy Review*, 45.4 (2012), pp. 483–505 <https://doi.org/10.1007/s11007-012-9232-y>

Puar, Jasbir, 'Prognosis Time: Towards a Geopolitics of Affect, Debility and Capacity', *Women & Performance: A Journal of Feminist Theory*, 19.2 (2009), pp. 161–72 <https://doi.org/10.1080/07407700903034147>

Putter, Ad, 'Finding Time for Romance: Mediaeval Arthurian Literary History', *Medium Aevum* 63 (1994), pp. 1–16 <http://doi.org/10.2307/43629612>

Quine, Willard Van Orman, 'Prefixes', in Quine, *Quiddities: An Intermittently Philosophical Dictionary* (Cambridge: Harvard University Press, 1987), pp. 162–65

Rabaté, Dominique, *Gestes lyriques* (Paris: José Corti, 2013)

—— 'A World of Gestures', *Journal of Literary Theory*, 11.1 (2017), special issue *Theories of Lyric*, ed. by Claudia Hillebrandt, Sonja Klimek, Ralph Müller, William Waters, and

Rüdiger Zymner, pp. 89–96 <https://doi.org/10.1515/jlt-2017-0010>

—— 'Énonciation poétique, énonciation lyrique', in *Figures du sujet lyrique*, ed. by Dominique Rabaté (Paris: PUF, 1996), pp. 65–79

Rajchman, John, '*Les Immatériaux* or How to Construct the History of Exhibitions', *Tate Papers*, 12 (2009) <https://www.tate.org.uk/research/publications/tate-papers/12/les-immateriaux-or-how-to-construct-the-history-of-exhibitions> [accessed 18 December 2018]

Rasch, William, 'Messias oder Katechon? Carl Schmitts Stellung zur politischen Theologie', in *Politische Theologie*, ed. by Jürgen Brokoff and Jürgen Fohrmann (Paderborn: Schöningh, 2003), pp. 39–54

Reeve, Daniel, 'Queer Arts of Failure in Hue of Rotelande and Alan of Lille', in *Medieval Thought Experiments: Poetry, Hypothesis, and Experience in the European Middle Ages*, ed. by Philip Knox, Jonathan Morton, and Daniel Reeve (Turnhout: Brepols, 2018), pp. 273–96

Riffaterre, Michael, *Semiotics of Poetry* (Bloomington: Indiana University Press, 1978)

Rilke, Rainer Maria, *Werke*, ed. by Manfred Engel, Ulrich Fülleborn, Horst Nalewski, and August Stahl, 4 vols. (Frankfurt a.M.: Insel, 1996), II: *Gedichte 1910 bis 1926*, ed. by Manfred Engel and Ulrich Fülleborn

Rose, Gillian, *Visual Metodologies: An Introduction to Researching with Visual Materials* (London: Sage, 2016)

Rotelande, Hue de, *Ipomedon, poème de Hue de Rotelande*, ed. by A. J. Holden (Paris: Klincksieck, 1979)

Rütinger, Ines, and Eva Schmidt, eds, *Dear Aby Warburg, What Can Be Done with Images?* (Heidelberg: Kehrer, 2012)

Scalise, Sergio, and Emiliano Guevara, 'The Lexicalist Approach to Word-Formation and the Notion of the Lexicon', in *Handbook of Word-Formation*, ed. by Pavol Štekauer and Rochelle Lieber (Dordrecht: Springer, 2005), pp. 147–87

Scherpe, Klaus R., and James Gussen, 'Reading the *Aesthetics of Resistance*: Ten Working Theses', *New German Critique*, 30 (Autumn 1983), pp. 97–105

Schmitt, Carl, *The Nomos of the Earth in the International Law of Jus Publicum Europaeum*, trans. by G. L. Ulmen (New York: Telos Press, 2006)

—— *Politische Theologie II: Die Legende von der Erledigung jeder Politischen Theologie* (Berlin: Duncker & Humblot, 1970), in English as *Political Theology II: The Myth of the Closure of Any Political Theology*, trans. and introduced by Michael Hoelzl and Graham Ward (Cambridge: Polity, 2008)

Schwartz, Jaime, 'Is a Photograph Still an Index If It's on the Internet?', *Dis Magazine* <http://dismagazine.com/discussion/41736/a-discursive-mask/> [accessed 18 December 2018]

Sebald, W. G., 'The Remorse of the Heart: On Memory and Cruelty in the Work of Peter Weiss', *On the Natural History of Destruction*, trans. by Anthea Bell (New York: Random House, 2003), pp. 169–91

Sedgwick, Eve Kosofsky, 'Paranoid Reading and Reparative Reading, or, You're So Paranoid, You Probably Think This Essay Is About You', in Sedgwick, *Touching Feeling: Affect, Pedagogy, Performativity* (Durham, NC: Duke University Press, 2003), pp. 123–51

Sekula, Allan, 'Between the Net and the Deep Blue Sea (Rethinking the Traffic in Photographs)', *October*, 102 (2002), pp. 3–34 <https://doi.org/10.1162/016228702320826434>

—— 'Reading an Archive: Photography Between Labour and Capital', in *The Photography Reader*, ed. by Liz Wells (London: Routledge, 2003), pp. 443–52

Semon, Richard, *Die Mneme als erhaltendes Princip im Wechsel des organischen Geschehens* (Leipzig: Engelmann, 1904)

Settis, Salvatore, ed., *Serial/Portable Classic: The Greek Canon and its Mutations* (Milan: Fondazione Prada, 2015)

Shildrick, Margrit, 'Border Crossings: The Technology of Disability and Desire', in *Culture, Theory, Disability: Encounters Between Disability Studies and Cultural Studies*, ed. by Anne Waldschmidt, Hanjo Berressem, and Moritz Ingwersen (Bielefeld: Transcript, 2017), pp. 137–51

Siebers, Tobin, *Disability Aesthetics* (Ann Arbor: University of Michigan Press, 2010)

Somaini, Antonio, and Andrea Pinotti, *Cultura visuale. Immagini, sguardi, media, dispositivi* (Turin: Einaudi, 2016)

Stählin, Wilhelm, 'Die Gestalt des Antichristen und das "katechon"', in *Festgabe Joseph Lortz*, ed. by Erwin Iserloh and

Peter Manns, 2 vols (Baden-Baden: Grimm, 1958), II: *Glaube und Geschichte*, pp. 1–12

Stewart, Susan, 'Preface to a Lyric History', in *The Uses of Literary History*, ed. by Marshall Brown (Durham, NC: Duke University Press, 1996)

Steyerl, Hito, 'Digital Debris: Spam and Scam', *October*, 138 (2011), pp. 70–80 <https://doi.org/10.1162/OCTO_a_00067>

—— 'In Defense of the Poor Image', in *The Wretched of the Screen* (Berlin: Sternberg Press, 2012), pp. 31–45

—— 'Politics of the Archive: Translations in Film', *transversal* (Vienna: eipcp, 2008) <http://eipcp.net/transversal/0608/steyerl/en> [accessed 18 December 2018]; repr. in Steyerl, *Beyond Representation: Essays 1999–2009*, ed. by Marius Babias (Berlin: n.b.k., 2016), pp. 160–66

—— 'Too Much World: Is the Internet Dead?', in *The Internet Does Not Exist*, ed. by Julieta Aranda, Brian Kuan Wood, and Anton Vidokle (Berlin: Sternberg Press, 2015), pp. 10–26

Stiker, Henri-Jacques, *The History of Disability* (Ann Arbor: University of Michigan Press, 1999)

Tadié, Jean-Yves, *Le Lac inconnu. Entre Proust et Freud* (Paris: Gallimard, 2012)

—— *Marcel Proust. Biographie*, 2 vols (Paris: Gallimard, 1996)

Taylor, Diana, *The Archive and the Repertoire: Performing Cultural Memory in the Americas* (Durham, NC: Duke University Press, 2003)

von Thurn und Taxis-Hohenlohe, Marie, *Erinnerungen an Rainer Maria Rilke* (Frankfurt a.M.: Insel, 1994)

Todorović, Jelena, *Dante and the Dynamics of Textual Exchange* (New York: Fordham University Press, 2016)

Tomiche, Anne, 'Anamnesis', in *Traversals of Affect*, ed. by J. Gaillard, C. Nouvet, and M. Stoholski, pp. 73–88

Trentin, Filippo, 'Warburg's Ghost: On Literary Atlases and the 'Anatopic' Shift of a Cartographic Object', in *De/Constituting Wholes: Towards Partiality Without Parts*, ed. by Manuele Gragnolati and Christoph F. E. Holzhey (Vienna: Turia + Kant, 2017), pp. 101–29

Vendler, Helen, *Poems, Poets, Poetry: An Introduction and Anthology* (Boston: Bedford/St. Martin's, 1997)

Wace, *Roman de Brut: A History of the British*, ed. and trans. by

Judith Weiss, rev. edn, Exeter Medieval Texts and Studies (Liverpool: Liverpool University Press, 2002)

Walsch, Raoul, *'daß wir nicht sehr verläßlich zu Haus sind in der gedeuteten Welt': Untersuchung zur Thematik der gedeuteten Welt in Rilkes 'Die Aufzeichnungen des Malte Laurids Brigge', 'Duineser Elegien' und spätester Lyrik* (Würzburg: Königshausen & Neumann, 2012)

Warburg, Aby, *Gesammelte Schriften*, ed. by Ulrich Pfisterer, Horst Bredekamp, Michael Diers, Uwe Fleckner, Michael Thimann, and Claudia Wedepohl (Berlin: Akademie Verlag, 1998–)

—— *Der Bilderatlas MNEMOSYNE*, in *Gesammelte Schriften*, II.1, ed. by Martin Warnke and Claudia Brink (2000), in Italian as *Mnemosyne. L'Atlante delle immagini*, ed. by Maurizio Ghelardi (Turin: Nino Aragno Editore, 2002)

—— *Fragmente zur Ausdruckskunde*, in *Gesammelte Schriften*, IV, ed. by Ulrich Pfisterer and Hans Christian Hönes (2015)

—— *Grundlegende Bruchstücke zu einer pragmatischen Ausdruckskunde. Frammenti sull'espressione*, ed. by Susanne Müller (Pisa: Edizioni della Normale, 2011)

—— 'A Lecture on Serpent Ritual', *Journal of the Warburg Institute*, 2 (1938–39), pp. 222–92

—— 'Pagan-Antique Prophecy in Words and Images in the Age of Luther', in *The Renewal of Pagan Antiquity* (1999), pp. 597–697

—— *The Renewal of Pagan Antiquity: Contributions to the Cultural History of the European Renaissance* (Los Angeles: Getty Center for the History of Art and the Humanities, 1999), in Italian as *La rinascita del paganesimo antico. Contributi alla storia della cultura* (Florence: La Nuova Italia, 1996); in English as

Weiss, Peter, *The Aesthetics of Resistance, Volume 1: A Novel*, trans. by Joachim Neugroschel (Durham, NC: Duke University Press, 2005)

—— *Marat/Sade*, trans. by Geoffrey Skelton and Adrian Mitchell (New York; Atheneum, 1983)

White, John J., 'History and Cruelty in Peter Weiss's "Marat/Sade"', *Modern Language Review*, 63.2 (1968), pp. 437–48

Wind, Edgar, 'On a Recent Biography of Warburg', in *The Eloquence of Symbols. Studies in Humanistic Art*, ed. by Jaynie

Anderson (Oxford: Oxford University Press, 1983), pp. 106–13

FILMOGRAPHY

Bojack Horseman, created by Raphael Bob-Waksberg (Netflix, 2014–)

Eye/Machine I, dir. by Harun Farocki (2000)

Full House, created by Jeff Franklin (ABC, 1987–1995)

Lorenza: Portrait of an Artist, dir. by Michael Stahlberg (Hochschule für Fernsehen und Film München, 1991) <https://vimeo.com/29793957> [accessed 10 December 2018]

Seinfeld, created by Larry David and Jerry Seinfeld (NBC, 1989–1998)

The Simpsons, created by Matt Groening (Fox Broadcasting, 1989–)

—— 'Bart Gets an Elephant', season 5, episode 17, dir. by Jim Reardon (aired 16 January 1994)

—— 'Bart vs. Australia', season 6, episode 16, dir. by Wes Archer (original air date: 19 February 1995)

—— 'Holidays of Future Passed', season 23, episode 9, dir. by Rob Oliver (aired 11 December 2011)

—— 'Mr. Lisa Goes to Washington', season 3, episode 2, dir. by Wes Archer (aired 26 September 1991)

—— 'The Two Mrs. Nahasapeemapetilons', season 9, episode 7, dir. by Steven Dean Moore (aired 16 November 1997)

—— 'Who Shot Mr. Burns?', season 6, episode 25, dir. by Jeffrey Lynch (aired 21 May 1995), and season 7, episode 1, dir. by Wes Archer (aired 17 September 1995)

—— 'You Only Move Twice', season 8, episode 2, dir. by Mike Anderson (aired 3 November 1996)

Notes on the Contributors

Cristina Baldacci is senior researcher at the Università Ca' Foscari, Venice. Her research interests focus on archive and atlas as visual forms of knowledge; appropriation, montage, and 're'-practices in contemporary art; sculpture and installation art. She is a convenor of the 'Re' Interdisciplinary Network (CRASSH, University of Cambridge) and part of the research group Global Art Archive (Departemento de Historia del Arte, Universitat de Barcelona). Her publications include the co-edited volumes *Quando è scultura* (2010), *Montages* (2018), *Abstraction Matters* (2019), and the monograph *Archivi impossibili* (2016).

Christiane Frey is an Alexander-von-Humboldt senior research fellow and has taught at New York University, Princeton University, the University of Chicago, and Konstanz University. Her research focuses on seventeenth- and eighteenth-century German literature in the European context. Her recent publications include *Laune. Poetiken der Selbstsorge von Montaigne bis Tieck* (2016) and the co-edited volume *Zu einer Poetik des Seriellen* (2016). Current research projects: 'The Time in Parenthesis: Constellations between Shakespeare and Gryphius', 'Micrologies of Knowledge from Bacon to Stifter', theories of secularization.

Julie Gaillard holds a Ph.D. in French from Emory University. Before joining the ICI Berlin as a Fellow (2016–18), she taught French language and literature at Emory University and Morehouse College. She is the co-editor of the volume *Traversals of Affect: On Jean-François Lyotard* (with Claire Nouvet and Mark Stoholski, 2016).

Francesco Giusti is currently affiliated with the ICI Berlin. After completing his PhD in Comparative Literature at Sapienza University of Rome and the Italian Institute of Human Sciences, he pursued his research on the history and theory of the lyric at the University of York and the Goethe-Universität Frankfurt. He has published two books, *Canzonieri in morte: Per un'etica poetica del lutto* (2015) and *Il desiderio della lirica: Poesia, creazione, conoscenza* (2016), and co-edited, with Christine Ott and Damiano Frasca, the volume *Poesia e nuovi media* (2018).

Clio Nicastro is an affiliated fellow at the ICI Berlin. After completing her PhD in Aesthetics and Theory of Arts at the University of Palermo, she moved to Berlin in 2015 as a DAAD fellow working on Harun Farocki. Her current research focuses on the cinematic representations of eating disorders as well as on cinema and labour, a project pursued in collaboration with Saima Akhtar and Rosa Barotsi since 2016.

Hannah Proctor works on histories and theories of radical psychiatry and emotional histories of the Left. She is currently working on a book called *Psychologies in Revolution: Alexander Luria, Soviet Subjectivities and Cultural History* for Palgrave Macmillan and another project on the psychic aftermath of political struggle.

Daniel Reeve holds a DPhil in English from the University of Oxford. He recently co-edited and contributed to *Medieval Thought Experiments: Poetry, Hypothesis and Experience in the European Middle Ages*. He currently teaches at Bard College Berlin.

Arianna Sforzini is a postdoctoral fellow for the ANR project 'Foucault's Reading Notes' (CNRS – ENS Lyon, 2018–20). She teaches philosophy and political theory at Sciences Po – Reims. She is a member of the *Centre Michel Foucault*, and has been an associated researcher at the *Bibliothèque nationale de France* (2016–17). She is the author of *Les Scènes de la vérité: Michel Foucault et le théâtre* (2017) and *Michel Foucault: Une pensée du corps* (2014).

Birkan Taş holds a BA in Psychology from Boğaziçi University in Istanbul and an MA in Cultural Studies from Istanbul Bilgi University. He received his PhD at the Amsterdam School for Cultural Analysis. His research interests encompass theories of gender and sexuality, the politics of temporality in disability and queer theory, and concepts of care and vulnerability in critical animal studies.

Tom Vandeputte is lecturer in continental philosophy and critical theory at the Sandberg Institute in Amsterdam, where he also directs the Critical Studies department. He completed his PhD at Goldsmiths College, University of London with the Centre for Philosophy and Critical Thought. Vandeputte's research focuses primarily on twentieth-century theories of language and history, in particular their implications and consequences for political thought.

Index

Cultural Inquiry

EDITED BY CHRISTOPH F. E. HOLZHEY AND MANUELE GRAGNOLATI

VOL. 8 MULTISTABLE FIGURES
On the Critical Potentials of Ir/Reversible Aspect-Seeing
Edited by Christoph F. E. Holzhey

VOL. 9 Wendy Brown / Rainer Forst
THE POWER OF TOLERANCE
Edited by Luca Di Blasi and Christoph F. E. Holzhey

VOL. 10 DENKWEISEN DES SPIELS
Medienphilosophische Annäherungen
Edited by Astrid Deuber-Mankowsky and Reinhold Görling

VOL. 11 DE/CONSTITUTING WHOLES
Towards Partiality Without Parts
Edited by Manuele Gragnolati and Christoph F.E. Holzhey

VOL. 12 CONATUS UND LEBENSNOT
Schlüsselbegriffe der Medienanthropologie
Edited by Astrid Deuber-Mankowsky and Anna Tuschling

VOL. 13 AURA UND EXPERIMENT
Naturwissenschaft und Technik bei Walter Benjamin
Edited by Kyung-Ho Cha

VOL. 14 LUCA DI BLASI
DEZENTRIERUNGEN
Beiträge zur Religion der Philosophie im 20. Jahrhundert

VOL. 15 RE-
An Errant Glossary
Edited by Christoph F. E. Holzhey and Arnd Wedemeyer

www.ingramcontent.com/pod-product-compliance
Lightning Source LLC
LaVergne TN
LVHW091411190726
843491LV00006B/1366

* 9 7 8 3 9 6 5 5 8 0 0 0 8 *